FIRST YOU DIE

LEARN TO LIVE AFTER
THE DEATH OF YOUR CHILD

To order additional copies, please contact us.
BookSurge, LLC
www.booksurge.com
1-866-308-6235
orders@booksurge.com

FIRST
YOU DIE

LEARN TO LIVE AFTER THE DEATH OF YOUR CHILD

by

Marie Levine

2004
Silver Thread Publishers

FIRST YOU DIE

LEARN TO LIVE AFTER
THE DEATH OF YOUR CHILD

CONTENTS

For Peter—

*Shaun, Adam & Karen, Mark, Ashley, Marco, Sam,
Leslie, Perry, Robert, Donald, Kareem & Kevin, Themis,
Tristan—and now Trevor, Theodore, Alexandra,
Ethelyne, Benjamin, Johnny Joe, Maureen, David, Brian,
Andrea, Ari, Ava, Neill, Michelle, Holden, Valerie,
Elizabeth, Dawn, Claudia, Adrienne, Andrew, Randy,
Jimmy, Daniel, Pierre, Anne Christina, Peter C., Jude,
Rowenna, Russell, Raphael, Raine, Alan,*

*and all the children I've come to know and love
—even in their absence.*

*And for all my caring compassionate friends, who shared
their stories and consoled me even while they bore the
burden of their own losses.*

*May they all find the courage and strength to relish the
remainder of their lives and look forward to being reunited
with our indelible children once more.*

ACKNOWLEDGEMENTS

In the earliest days of my journey, the only place I could go to vent, to cry, to rave or to wail at the heavens was my journal. In time, I felt brave enough to share my thoughts with similarly afflicted friends . . . those who had also survived this loss. From the moment I began writing publicly, these compassionate friends came forward to thank me for capturing their own thoughts and encouraging me to keep writing.

Carol Gertz and Eileen Mitzman were the first to insist that I put together a book of my columns, so that those who follow on this path can be comforted in the knowledge they are not alone.

Maddie Kasden, Genesse Gentry and Jan McNess, whose broken hearts are revealed in poetry and words that speak volumes about the "condition" of bereaved parenthood, generously agreed to let me share a few of my favorites with you.

Molly Fumia, whose book, <u>Safe Passage</u>, became my bible during my darkest days.

To Pat Antich, Barbara Berkall, Sandi & Harvey Schneider, Jacquie Mitchell, Nancy Wight, and all my treasured compassionate friends, who have encouraged me in this decade-long effort.

To Dr. Barbara Chasen, an extraordinary woman who, in spite of her pain, reached out into the world to recover a lost life, and invited me to share the experience . . . two broken hearts now joined in an effort to build an unimaginable future.

To Tom Cozine, a gift from the gods, who serendipitously came into our lives, a seeming replica of our lost son. It is through Tom, a young man with a giant heart, who has shared the trials and tribulations of his young life, that we can imagine what life might have been like if Peter had lived.

To Judy Block, Linda Kaye Wilson, Jane Tucker Radley, Nancy & Neil Breslau, the late Rita Angelo, Myra Frost and all my "civilian" friends who were there for me and whose caring, loving friendship and patience never wavered during my long, dark nights.

To James Van Praagh, a world-renowned psychic medium, and best-selling author, who convinced me that life does go on, and who has become my friend in the process.

And a special thank you to Dorothy Jordon, a most compassionate and generous friend who, with some help from her wonderful husband, David Ferber, spent practically her whole grieving first year editing, affirming and re-creating this collection of essays into what we hope will offer some small measure of comfort and solace to those who must also make this journey. As Dorothy says, "Working on this book helped me so much during this past year. Feelings and emotions I couldn't articulate were untangled for me, and, when I was most despairing, Marie's words gave me hope. No other book

I read during this first awful year offered me that prospect—
which is so integral to <u>First You Die</u>."

It is *my* hope that this book can offer the same modicum
of comfort to those who must also travel this painful path,
as they struggle to incorporate their grief into a life the they
could never have imagined, but one that can become rich in
compassion, memory and love.

The Compassionate Friends, referred to extensively in this book, is an international non-profit organization that assists families toward the positive resolution of grief following the death of a child of any age and provides information to help others to be supportive.

The world's largest self-help bereavement organization, **The Compassionate Friends** has nearly six hundred chapters serving all fifty states and a presence in approximately twenty-nine countries.

More than fifteen thousand people attend local chapter meetings, and outreach is provided to more than two hundred thousand bereaved families and professionals each month in the United States.

For more information, log onto
<u>www.thecompassionatefriends.org</u>
or call, toll-free, 1-877-969-0010.

"Who better to soften the wound of another,
than one who has suffered the wound himself"?

—*Thomas Jefferson*

INTRODUCTION

On August 7th 1993, three days after landing his first "real" job, three weeks after turning 22, and three months after graduating from Syracuse University, my son Peter was killed in a violent automobile accident. He was being driven home by one of his college friends. The driver and the other two young men in the car were only slightly bruised. Peter died instantly.

Peter was our only child. My husband Phil and I had no grieving sibling to attend to. In some way this provided us the "luxury" of coming to grips with the unfathomable loss of our lives unencumbered by any other's needs.

During those first drowning days, torn between the longing to simply die and the instinct to survive, I found **The Compassionate Friends** (TCF), an international bereavement group (with almost 600 chapters in the United States) exclusively for parents who have lost a child, and for surviving siblings. The first TCF meeting I attended left me less than comforted. In fact, I found it so unsettling I decided not to return. I know now that some parents find immediate consolation. Not me. The meeting left me feeling even more despondent (if that was possible). However, I was encouraged to return several months later and, after that second TCF meeting, the group became my lifeline. An irrepressible journaler, writing had become my best form of therapy. Before long I began to edit TCF's Manhattan Chapter newsletter, which eventually led to my writing a regular "column."

ABOUT THIS BOOK

This is not a "How to" book nor is it a book that must be read cover to cover, a continuum that will be appreciated only in the order it is assembled. Similar to the process of grieving, this book is comprised of feelings experienced in the jumbled order of grief itself. It is my hope that readers can pick up and open the book to almost any page and hopefully find some solace in recognizing and relating to the familiar experiences all bereaved parents share.

Much has been written in recent years about the process of grieving, both by professionals and those who have experienced it. Those who find themselves in the midst of this experience can find a great deal of very helpful material designed to offer comfort and healing, and guidance.

Simply put, this is the story of one mother's experience. Of starting at what was the end of one life, and finding the beginnings of another. There's no advice within these pages. I only relate the emotions I felt as I traveled on a (too) well-worn path of pain and suffering that so many mothers have traveled before me—and that others will continue to navigate.

Grieving the loss of a child is a unique experience. It doesn't matter that it has happened to countless millions before. Nothing and no one can prepare a parent for the ensuing emotional roller coaster. Each experience is exclusive, yet so universal. It doesn't matter that every bereaved parent that has gone before has run the gamut of identical emotions. We must each discover the nuance of every feeling by ourselves. Being alerted to what lies ahead only reassures us that we aren't losing our minds. We still must go it alone. Only in looking back as we traverse this difficult path do we find comfort in recognizing that what we feel has been felt before by all those who are ahead of us.

Throughout this book I've woven the columns I've written for our Compassionate Friends newsletter over the course of nine years, as well as some of the writings and poetry that brought me comfort on my journey. It is my hope that readers will find some consolation in these pages.

This is one mother's story. I tell it understanding that it mirrors the experience of countless bereaved parents everywhere.

Marie Levine

CHAPTER 1: AT FIRST YOU DIE

OTHER PEOPLE

Every so often,
you hear about other people
losing their child.
Sometimes there is a horrible accident
you find out about on television.
Sometimes it is a senseless murder or suicide
you read about in the newspaper.
Sometimes you learn about a deadly illness over
the telephone because, this time,
the child belongs to someone you know.

When such a tragedy happens,
to other people,
your heart goes out to them.
You feel deeply saddened and, perhaps,
you shed a few tears.
You then continue your charmed life,
going about business as usual.
You don't forget, but,
you don't necessarily remember either.
After all, the death of a child
is something that occurs in the lives
of other people.

Unless, God forbid,
the television story or newspaper article or
telephone call
is about your child.
Unless, one terrible day,
heaven and earth and hell become one.
Unless your life loses all meaning and
nothing makes sense anymore.
Suddenly,
by a random twist of fate, or the hand of God,
you have become other people.

Madelaine Perri Kasden
Written In Loving Memory of Her Son,
Neill Perri, 10/2/71-6/15/95

THE PHONE CALL

The unthinkable—every parent's nightmare—happened on a rainy Friday night while visiting my sister and her family in California. It had been a long day, the end of my vacation. My sister and I had spent the day in Carmel and, although my niece was throwing a farewell party for my nephew who was leaving for graduate school back east the next day, we were exhausted and chose to stay home to watch a movie before turning in early.

Just past 9 p.m. the phone rang.

My brother-in-law answered the phone while my sister adjusted the volume on the video. I had seen the movie before so I told her to let it run while I went to take the call. Annoyed at my husband, with whom I had been quarrelling when I left New York the week before (and hadn't spoken to since), I picked the receiver up off the desk and icily said, "Hello."

"Sweetheart," he said, "I need you to be brave."

"What's wrong?" I countered, immediately fearing that one of the cats we had recently adopted had fallen out of a window.

"Please be brave," he insisted.

"What's wrong?" I demanded, my voice rising impatiently.

"There's been an accident."

"What happened?"

"Peter's been in an accident."

Still my mind held. "Is he okay?" I couldn't stand it any longer. What was taking him so long to get to the point?

"He died instantly," came the reply.

I remember screaming, "Nooooooooooooooo . . ."

I remember everything because, at that moment, my mind separated from my body and floated up to the ceiling where it remained—impersonally recording the next several hours—as I flailed about helplessly screaming in an agony of madness, trying desperately to force my body to shatter into the million pieces that my mind already had.

In New York, Phil remained holding the phone, listening. Those who have been through similar experiences know what happened then. There is nothing neat and tidy about the discovery of the sudden death of your child. As I screamed and rolled around on the floor, smashing my head repeatedly against the floor, the furniture, anything . . . my sister and her husband tried desperately to contain me.

Somehow, I was able to learn the facts. The accident had taken place at 2 a.m. New York time. Peter had gone out Friday night with some of his college buddies who were in the city from Connecticut for the evening. Though it was raining, Peter was bored, forced to stay in town for the weekend because of a job interview instead of joining friends in Saratoga as originally planned.

At the end of an evening of partying in Manhattan, driving in the rain, Peter was seated behind the driver. There were four young men in the car. When the speeding car lost control just blocks from our home, and went careening from one side of the highway to the other, Peter was cast out through the rear window like a rocket, the boy next to him following close behind. But it was Peter who broke the window and died instantly. The other three walked away physically unscathed.

Phil had received the call from the police Saturday morning, and had to absorb the news alone. While in a fog of disbelief and tortuous agony, the police took him to the medical examiners office—what can only be imagined as a living nightmare—to identify the body of our only child. He then spent the day interviewing the surviving young men and trying to figure out how to breathe. Deciding to allow me one last day, he made a conscious decision not to call me until day's end. By the time I got the call in California, with a time difference of three hours, Peter had been dead 22 hours . . . I never suspected a thing.

At some point my voice gave out, but even that didn't stop me from screaming. The screaming continued incessantly but now there was no sound. Just air and pathetic squeaking as I ripped at my hair and begged to go home . . . crawling toward the door as if I could be transported home simply by my desperate need to be there.

By midnight my brother-in-law had made arrangements for my sister and me to be on the first plane out the next morning. Exhausted, and wrapped in a blanket, I sat up all night in the living room trying to absorb the news, while my sister and her husband lay down to grab a few brief hours of sleep before facing the rest of our lives.

In the morning, I somehow had the presence of mind to give my brother-in-law the names of a few friends to call. My sister then accompanied me home. All the way to the airport, on the plane, in the taxi, we traveled to my home in New York in silence. I couldn't utter a word until I walked into my apartment and faced Phil who, on our living room table, had already created a little memorial to Peter.

Now, finally, almost 24 hours after Phil called me, after almost two days alone in the apartment, Phil and I were together, the only two people on the planet that felt the full magnitude of this calamity. Phil burst into tears, adding more details. I found it all impossible to believe, no less understand.

Sitting numbly on the sofa, trying to wrap my flickering mind around the details, I was stunned when my friend Jane (one of those I had instructed my brother-in-law to call) suddenly came rushing into the house, raced over and sat at my feet. She wrapped her arms around my legs and put her head on my lap. I will never forget that simple gesture of love and compassion. During the next several years I would look back to that moment many times in wonder, as I was forced to deal with the many disappointing responses of so many of the people I looked helplessly to for support and understanding.

There would be plenty of time to question, reflect, wonder, grieve and mourn. Now there were ceremonies to get through and arrangements to be made. Unable to make a sound more than a hoarse whisper, I began making funeral preparations. Convinced I had little time to live—after all, how could I go on without Peter—it became important that I complete these arrangements and get my own life in order before I expired. For surely I knew I would die. So much of me already had.

DEALING WITH GRIEF

Much has been written about the stages of grief—all of it neatly organized so that the grievers, and those who attempt to support them, can get a handle on the ups and downs of the impending roller coaster ride that this emotional devastation brings. While it's true that these explanations and descriptions can serve as some kind of road map to grieving, as in any destination—ours being "coming to terms," or "accepting," or "getting on with life" (all hateful phrases)—there are so many ways to get there and, once there, so many places to explore. We may never be totally familiar with the new landscape. And whenever you think you know your way around, something unexpected appears and you must find your way back to safety. As we all know, many get lost along the way and some never stop to see how far they've traveled.

Ultimately we, the grieving, become isolated travelers, as those who began the journey with us grow tired or impatient with our search for a place that the uninitiated cannot envision. Hopefully, on the way, we meet other travelers seeking the same destination. The comfort we get from those who totally understand our confusion—because they too share the same fate—becomes our lifeline and they our lifetime companions.

For me, the experience of losing Peter (in my case our only child) has been as life altering an experience as having been diagnosed with a terminal illness. Absorbing this new reality into my personality has become a daily effort. Some people make it look easy to the uninitiated. But to those on the journey, the effort is heroic.

My journey began in 1993, just as I was about to release my child into the world. I had nurtured Peter and he had grown into a splendid young adult. I was confident he had learned the lessons necessary to begin his life on his own. I was prepared to sit back and watch as he flew out of the nest, returning to entertain me with a lifetime of his experiences that would remind me of my own so many years before. It was the next stage in the natural progression of our lives.

Peter was the natural recipient of my and Phil's gene pool. We had labored for 22 years and fully expected to watch Peter, imbued as he was with our values, take these tools and better the world he was about to inherit.

But it was not to be.

GETTING OVER "IT" . . .
Fall 1996

As we all continue to move numbly through our lives, all of us sharing this same unspeakable experience . . . though some continue to try to measure the uniqueness of their experience as opposed to another's . . . we do all find ourselves confronted with a universal desire on the part of the uninitiated. Namely, are we getting over it?

When a recently bereaved parent comes up against this question, the response is generally an insufficient one. For how do we respond to such a question? After all, we have been getting over things all of our lives. Our first punishment, an illness, a bruise or a scrape, a failed grade. Later, a lost friendship, a lost love, a missed experience. As life becomes more complicated the losses grow in proportion: A failed marriage; life-threatening illness; financial calamity; job loss; the loss of a parent, a friend. Somehow, we manage to survive all these losses. It's part of life we are told. Given time, we will get over it. In most cases, undeniably true. We do.

Given these shared experiences, we know in our hearts that time heals. But how do we respond to those who, in their misguided effort to comfort us in our pitifully bereaved state, continue to assure us that we will get over it, or ask plaintively of others, "Is she/he getting over it yet?" How do we tell them that this is one wound that continues to throb for all of time?

The fact is that we cannot. It is not possible for anyone not here in this place to even slightly comprehend the mystery of this pain. How we can spend longer and longer periods of "evenness" and then, from out of nowhere, a tidal wave of emotion will blindside us. Walking down the street, in an elevator, the supermarket, waiting in line, at a meeting . . .

No, getting over it depends on the "it." This "it" is too unspeakable, too unbelievable, too over the edge to get over. It is too high, too wide, too deep to get over, under, around or through. We are trapped forever within it. It is who we are. It is who we have become. It is a life sentence that condemns us, and at the same time, challenges us to survive.

And we do. We go on. We wake up every morning and engage in the ordinary activities of the day. When those same misguided sages, with nothing more in their minds or hearts than the moment they are in, tell us we must get on with our lives, we can look them in the eye and assure them that we are. With the overbearing weight of our emotional burden, we do go on, living memorials to our children and to all the bereaved parents who came before us . . . and who we, in our own innocence back then, hoped would someday be able to get over "it."

CHAPTER 2: THE FIRST YEAR

THE BEGINNING

My story is about one mother's surviving the loss of a young man who had managed to complete his childhood. As a young adult, his manhood was before him. He was all future and little past. My husband and I, on the other hand, were just about complete. We had survived the hard part and were set to safely launch our fledgling. For us, it seemed the rest would be easy. We'd sit back, watch him marry, dance at his wedding, greet our grandchildren, retire happily, travel the world . . . nothing but blue horizons. Needless to say, in our vision, there was only good health, good fortune and good times. We certainly were dreamers.

Life as we knew it ended on August 7, 1993. Our new life began about a year later: After the funeral. After the traditional week of mourning. After the caring, kind visits of friends and family. After the consoling phone calls. After the first month anniversary, the first Yom Kippur, the first Thanksgiving, the first Christmas, the first New Year's Eve. After the first Valentine's Day, Passover, Spring. After the first warm day filled with the promise of renewal. Memorial Day. Summer. After the first birthday and dreaded anniversary day. After the first year without Peter. That first year was filled with so many dreaded days of anticipated commemoration.

That first year no one expected anything of us. The phone calls were still laden with the determined concern of friends and family. It was only at the beginning of year two that it became clear to us that we would not die. Somehow we were condemned to survive, relegated to living in this terminally bereaved state forever.

It also became clear that those who had supported us for a year were now expecting to see some evidence of healing. From my perspective however, nothing had changed. The world was still dark and grey. My despair was as palpable as ever. My ability to "move on" was non-existent. I was as despondent as ever—and more alone as support faded.

During the earliest days I remained in shock. My brain couldn't absorb as much information as it needed to process. My mind had shut down after making funeral arrangements. It took every ounce of my energy to simply make it through each minute of each day.

I knew there was a lot to think about but I also recognized that I had lost the ability to prioritize my thoughts. I knew that I was on unfamiliar ground and that I needed to try and understand what had happened. Yet, every breath was difficult. Sleep became my great escape.

The first day that I was alone, I embarked to the nearest bookstore, found the section on *Death & Dying*, sat on the floor and began reading. I was still reading when darkness fell outside. I felt this urgent need to become familiar with death. For how could my child know so much more about it than I did?

Day after day I returned to the bookstore. I tried to compare what I was reading with the way I was feeling. I waited for each of the "stages of grief"—at times suspecting that I was stuck in one when I should have moved on to the next. The disbelief was incessant. That Peter was no longer on this planet, walking these streets, seeing the same people, hearing the same noises, tasting the same foods, experiencing the same days was impossible to imagine. Weeping uncontrollably 10 or 20 times a day . . . always in the morning, in the shower, on the bus, in the car, on the street, in a store, and in the evening, before dinner, after dinner, at bedtime . . . I spent weeks thanking everyone who had attended his funeral or sent a note. Every thank you had to have Peter's picture on it. Everyone had to have an imprint of my beautiful son.

Then came the books. For a year I labored over small keepsake books filled with pictures of Peter with each of the individual recipients . . . each of his friends, my niece, my nephew, his aunt, his fraternity . . . the huge photo portrait, framed with a brass plaque, to hang in his fraternity house for all of time

One thing that was clear to me, even then, was that I could not let Peter die. I could live only to assure his memory. It was an insanely driven effort. Within days I had contacted Syracuse University (he had graduated only three months before the accident) to ask them to stop the presses on his yearbook. They had to wait while I created a memorial page so that anyone looking at the yearbook from the class of 1993 would think, even briefly, about Peter.

Days later, Phil and I decided to start a scholarship in his name, and this became my driving force. I contacted his high school to establish a fund, talking with them about Peter and the criteria that would be used to grant an award. This was followed by a fundraising appeal. My letters had to bear Peter's picture so that I knew that for a few seconds every recipient would be thinking of him when they learned of our efforts.

As time went on, another fundraising appeal letter would go out around the holidays each year, complete with a picture of Peter and that year's recipient of the award that bore his name. Lovingly written, addressed, stamped, mailed . . . these efforts kept me thinking about all the people who would once again have thoughts of Peter prance across their consciousness.

Keeping Peter's memory alive became my reason for living. While despairing thoughts of being released from this life continued to cross my mind, Phil's pleas, assuring me that as long as I lived, Peter would live gave me the motivation I needed to persevere. I didn't know how I would manage but, if my living would keep my son present in this world, I would stay on.

AND YET THIS HAPPENED TO ME

I took motherhood so seriously
I took nothing for granted
I was always thankful
for what I had,
and yet this happened to me.

I chose to stay with them,
live through their lives closely,
put my own aspirations

on hold 'til they'd grown,
and still, this happened to me.

My life was spent caring
for two lovely daughters
who made my life special
in so many ways.

One day she was living,
alive, well and thriving.
The next she was gone
to a life we can't share.

I'm learning to struggle
through life and the grieving,
to find ways of being
that bring wholeness and peace,
and live with what happened to me.

Genesse Gentry from her book <u>Stars in the Deepest Night</u>

ALIEN THOUGHTS . . .
Summer 1996

I was struck the other day by a morning TV show hostess (who shall remain nameless) who, while interviewing a resident of Dunblaine, Scotland, asked solemnly, "How are the families doing now, eight weeks after that awful day? Are they recovering from such a terrible and tragic event?"

What on earth was she thinking? Recovering? Obviously civilian thoughts. Civilians need desperately to be reassured that survivors of their dead children can indeed recover. A few months ago we acknowledged the first anniversary of the Oklahoma City bombing. News shows, talk shows, magazines, newspapers . . . all rushed to commemorate the hoped for closing chapter of this deadly story. But we know better.

Now we have TWA Flight 800. Every day television introduces us to hordes of newly indoctrinated aliens. For surely those of us who bury our children become members of an "other" class of earthbound inhabitants . . . the terminally bereaved. Those who seem to beg for assurance that we can indeed "recover" from this condition are intent on this assurance to assuage their fear, for they know they are just as vulnerable as we were when we were snatched from our cozy, normal lives.

A sniper here, a plane crash there, a drug overdose, a drunk driver, a gas explosion, a train wreck, an electrical fire, unprotected sex, an inability to cope, a rear end collision, a speeding car on a rain slicked highway, a misguided terrorist, a disgruntled ex-coworker, an undiagnosed virus, a stroke, an aneurysm, cancer . . . skiing, roller blading, jet skiing . . . so many ways to die. Some sinister, some innocent . . . all a surprise.

The newscaster asks, with a heavy dose of rehearsed sympathy, "How are you coping with this tragedy?" The numbed survivor barely knows how to respond. The truth is they are not "coping." They are marveling at their own survival. It is unimaginable to survive such an unspeakable loss. How can we describe such a dark place to this interviewer who, no matter how intent on trying to understand, is biologically incapable of comprehending this particular unknown.

But we now know. We travel through this deadly landscape and find each other among the ruins of our lives. We cling to each other and find the strength to endure and go on. We become living monuments to our lost children and learn to live out our lives. We reach out to the newcomers. We do understand. We don't just remember. We continue to feel, with each new arrival, the intensity of our own early pain. And that pain makes us feel our children present.

And none of us really want to move away from that.

FINDING THE COMPASSIONATE FRIENDS

"Without friends the world is but a wilderness. There is no man that imparteth his joy to his friends, but that he joyeth more, and no man that imparteth grief to his friends but he grieveth the less."

Frances Bacon

So much has been written about the experience of losing a child . . . the shock, the anger, the pain, the guilt, the disbelief—a litany of emotions. For me, the focus in those first months was on the pain . . . not only the emotional pain, but the unremitting physical pain of my heart hurting, or the headaches, backaches and the countless voluntary infections that attacked my now vulnerable body. Even my teeth began to migrate causing huge spaces to appear between them. Then, the confusion of disconnected thoughts that began popping into my head, making me think I was losing my mind. And always the guilt . . . the "what ifs," the "if onlys," the "whys."

I remembered so many of the people who came to see me that first week, whispering in my ear that I should seek help. I was very numb and agreeable to everyone's advice. The truth was that I could barely breathe, let alone figure out what help to get.

Four weeks after Peter was killed, I heard about a support group called The Compassionate Friends. I remember thinking that it was an unwieldy name for an organization. But its focus was on grieving parents. People who had buried their children. I decided to go to a meeting even though Phil decided not to come with me. Still in shock and disbelieving this could be happening to us, seeming to be dragging my brains along behind me, I ventured out alone to a local church where this monthly meeting was held.

Greeted at the door by a few very genial people, I was asked what had happened and, when I managed to get the words out, received a gentle hug from a total stranger who then volunteered that he had been through a similar experience three years earlier. I remember thinking at the time that certainly after three years this gentleman was probably close to being "over it." I also suspected that he couldn't possibly have had the same intensity of emotion for his son as I had for mine. After all, he was smiling and totally comfortable telling me his story.

At the meeting there were lots of books on the subject of grieving the loss of children. I helped myself to two of them. When it was time for the meeting to begin, the group leader made some announcements, described how the meeting would progress, and then, sitting in a large circle, the 30 or 40 people in the room began to introduce themselves and tell about their loss. I was dumbstruck that all of these people, chatting and smiling to each other only moments before, were now admitting that they had suffered the death of a child, some within the preceding year, some years before. Children of all ages dying from car accidents, illness, drugs, AIDS, murder, suicide . . . and the deaths from such seemingly innocent causes . . . swimming, biking, skiing, roller-blading. How was it possible that so much contained horror could be right before my eyes. One woman, barely able to speak, told of losing her 12-year-old son just seven days before. It had taken me 30 days to muster up the strength and courage to check out this group. How had she, in all her despair and disbelief, managed to drag herself to this place only seven days later?

And what in the world were we all here looking for? Surely we didn't expect to feel better. We weren't hoping to drown our sorrows and blank out our memories. We weren't looking for comfort for we knew we didn't want to be placated.

It was years before I understood that drowning in despair, we all sought a lifeline. Something we could grab on to while our world rocked crazily out of control. Ultimately, I recognized that managing the pain was what it would take to survive.

The pain of having lost a child defies description. Because there are no words to adequately describe all the feelings, most of us learn to speak in metaphor. We liken the discomfort to images we can describe. It is probably why so many of those who experience this calamity become prolific writers. The written word lends itself to metaphor so much more than the spoken word.

During those first months I was reading all that I could find, and so much of what I read reached out to me in ways that no spoken words could. It was through the poetry and prose of the mortally bereaved that I recognized so much of what I was feeling, and I found a measure of comfort in discovering how others described my own altered state.

ALWAYS YESTERDAY
Fall 2000

The first time I walked into a meeting of The Compassionate Friends, I had been a bereaved parent for four weeks. Some of the people who greeted me had been at it for two or three years. I remember one person who had been bereaved for five years, and I think now about some of the thoughts that went through my mind then. That someone who was two years ahead of me was so beyond feeling what I was feeling . . . why, I thought, they're practically over it. Three years was further along than I could possibly imagine, and five years . . . well, five years. What were they doing there?

A few days ago I spoke to a friend whom I met during those first weeks. Her brother had died three years earlier and she was so broken hearted for me then. We bonded as bereaved people do and our friendship has flourished. The other day, she was tenderly commiserating with me as we contemplated the upcoming 7th anniversary of Peter's death and the 10th anniversary of her brother's. And what we realized as we spoke is that although we've come a long way, there is no time after the death of a child . . . or a sibling. In our world, it's always yesterday.

I've been in survival mode now for seven years. I've learned a lot. I've learned some of the coping skills I need to live my life. I've learned to live with Peter as a more present aspect of my life then he might have been if he lived thousands of miles away. He is in my consciousness every minute. I've learned that no matter what the experts say about being a bereaved parent . . . no one has figured out how to describe the reality of our world. I've also learned how important it is to try. And I've learned that I will continue to learn how to go on. That I have no more answers about my life now than I did when Peter was alive. But I do have more questions.

I think about that first year a lot. I remember:

—   *waking up every day to discover the nightmare was real, sobbing uncontrollably at the reality,*
—   *feeling a genuine hollow emptiness just below my heart,*
—   *moving in slow motion,*
—   *the "whys," "what ifs" and "if onlys,"*
—   *the torment of feeling he was going through the same struggle on the other side,*
—   *forgetting to breathe . . . then suddenly gasping for air,*

— *becoming lost in thought and discovering almost a whole day had gone by,*
— *feeling like the world was out of sync, like a movie slightly off its soundtrack,*
— *wondering, wondering how I could possibly survive and not even wanting to,*
— *feeling singularly punished by fate,*
— *wanting to feel "better" but not wanting to let go of the intensity of my pain,*
— *seeing any eventual healing as a betrayal of my love for Peter,*
— *fearing that people would judge my behavior as a reflection of how much I hurt or didn't hurt— knowing how much I always hurt,*
— *being angry at all the platitudes directed at me: "Time heals . . . ," "He's in a better place . . . ," "You need to get on with your life . . . ," and my favorite; "You're so unbelievable. If it were me, I would die!"*

How was that supposed to make me feel? Did it mean they loved their children more? That their pain would be great enough to kill? That mine wasn't enough? Truth is, that's what I always thought when I heard about someone else. And that's the big revelation. We don't die. We go on, forced to learn a whole new way to cope with a totally new, unimaginable life.

I vividly remember my physical discomfort that first year. Uncomfortable in my own skin, desperate for some magical, impossible comfort, a release from my torment. Even while I feared losing that same pain. And I remember my anger— anger at the event, anger at my victimization, anger at those who tried to comfort me . . . anger at those who didn't. Surviving those first few years are as surprising as the event itself. It amazes me to this day that we continue to live our lives. Indeed, we even make plans!

Today, Peter is still on my mind every minute. But every minute is not filled with unmitigated pain and disbelief. That only happens sometimes. Most of the time I think of him with a smile, remembering what a wonder he was. I speak of him all the time, determined that he remain a part of this life.

Now I know what every bereaved parent before me knew—and what all those who will come after will learn: That there is no way we ever forget. That we'll never "get better" or "get over it." That our children are with us every minute. That not a holiday, birthday, or anniversary goes by without our noting their absence. That every day we wonder what they would be doing now.

That no matter how far we travel on this journey, when we think of our children, it seems like just yesterday.

CHAPTER 3: MEN AND WOMEN

MEN DO CRY

I heard quite often that "men don't cry"
Though no one ever told me why.
So when I fell and skinned a knee
No one came to comfort me.

And when some bully boy at school
Would pull a prank so mean and cruel
I'd quickly learn to turn and quip
"It doesn't hurt"—and bite my lip.

So as I grew to reasoned years
I learned to stifle all my tears.
Though "Be a big boy" it began,
Quite soon I learned to "be a man."

And I could play that stoic role
While storm and tempest wracked my soul
Neither pain nor setback could there be
To wrest one single tear from me.

Then one night I stood nearby
And hopelessly watched my son die.
And quickly found (to my surprise)
That all the "tearless talk" was lies.

And I still cry and have no shame
I cannot play that "big boy" game.
And openly, without remorse,
I let my sorrow take its course.

So those of you who can't abide
A man you've seen who's often cried,
Reach out to him with all your heart
As one whose life's been torn apart.

For men do cry when they can see
Their loss of immortality.
And tears will come in endless streams,
When mindless fate destroys their dreams.

Ken Falk

It soon became clear to me that Phil and I were grieving very differently. While I felt totally incapacitated, except for my efforts to memorialize Peter, Phil needed to immerse himself in work. Having spent my entire adult life working very energetically, and actively participating in the business world, I now felt as if I was living under water.

Waking up was almost impossible. Getting out of bed seemed to take forever. Dressing so exhausted me I would need to rest afterwards. Unaware of time, I would disappear into my daydreams and "come to" hours later to find the day almost over. Venturing out of the house was barely possible. A walk to the bookstore, just a few blocks away, took hours. People passing me in the street must have thought I was catatonic.

Meanwhile, Phil went to work and spent evenings crying into his pillow. I railed at the heavens and wept audibly all day. As part of my new routine I read the obituaries and, whenever I read about a young person with surviving parents, I would try to locate them and write to them. I recognized early on that I was now "different."

Like an alien on another planet, I took to calling all bereaved parents aliens. For we were now forced to live amongst the "living," whose futures were still intact, while we had to carefully navigate unfamiliar terrain and figure out how to make do with the remains of our lives. I began to feel angry towards everyone because I knew they couldn't possibly understand all that I was feeling. I surely didn't have the patience or the wherewithal to try to teach them. I only wanted to be around other bereaved parents whom I knew could understand the depth of my pain, even while dealing with their own.

So many people in those days thought they were helpful when they suggested that many marriages dissolved after experiencing the death of a child. I wasn't sure if they were trying to be helpful by warning me of the possibility. There were even imaginary statistics tossed out implying that as many as 75% of marriages were ultimately doomed by this calamity.

Such stunning declarations were finally clarified in June 1999 when The Compassionate Friends commissioned a study that showed this figure to be the myth that it is. Surely many marriages dissolve as a result of all the additional pressures often placed on marriage partners to grieve according to another's style or schedule or a need to place blame for the event. However, the study, conducted by NFO Research, Inc.

on behalf of The Compassionate Friends, Inc., was clear in its findings. Following is an excerpt:

GRIEF AND DIVORCE

Newly bereaved parents frequently read or hear disturbing statistics about a high divorce rate (often claimed to be 80-90%) among couples following the death of a child. However, TCF has never found reliable statistics concerning divorce rates following the death of a child.

To confirm or refute these claims, the survey included a series of questions regarding marital status. Based on the results, it is clear that the divorce rates quoted so often are erroneous. Overall, 72% of parents who were married at the time of their child's death are still married to the same person. The remaining 28% of marriages include 16% in which one spouse had died, and only 12% of marriages that ended in divorce.

While this percent may be slightly understated due to sample composition, the undoubted conclusion is that the divorce rate among bereaved parents is significantly below the often-cited numbers, and may in fact be lower than the level in the population in general. Furthermore, even among the 12% of parents whose marriages ended in divorce, only one out of four of them felt that the impact of the death of their child contributed to their divorce.

The complete study can be found on the TCF website at www.compassionatefriends.org.

More often, in my experience, it seems the calamitous death of a child results in the parents being driven towards each other for comfort, recognizing that only the other parent has experienced an almost identical loss. Who but the mother and father, who are closest to the pain, can understand and try to relieve the emotional devastation each one is feeling.

While I was feeling disordered emotional devastation, Phil described what he was feeling as humiliation. At first, I couldn't understand what he was trying to tell me. Then I realized that the pitying looks and helpless comments of his co-workers made him feel victimized. Like so many men, talking about feelings had never come naturally to Phil. Now, with life's most irreverent blow finding its mark on our little family, Phil turned inward and focused his energy on keeping me whole.

Like two beached whales, struggling to survive in an environment neither of us knew, we clumsily took turns consoling each other, knowing all too well that our efforts were producing negligible results. But we did have each other. We were the only two people on the planet who knew Peter equally well and bore the same scars from losing him.

No matter how Phil did or didn't express his pain, I had no doubt he was as intensely wounded as I was. He, more than anyone, understood the measure of my grief. He looked for no reassurance from me that I was feeling "better." He knew from his own internal barometer that no matter how I appeared, I had shattered into a million pieces just as he had. Barely glued together, we were always on the verge of cracking and crumbling. We "handled" each other as if we were made of eggshells. Which indeed, we were.

NEVERNESS

*It's the neverness that is so painful.
Never again to be here with us—never
to sit with us at the table, never to
travel with us, never to laugh with us,
never to cry with us, never to embrace us
as he leaves for school, never to see his
brothers and sister marry. All the rest of
our lives we must live without him. Only
our death can stop the pain of his
death. A month, a year, five years . . .
with that I could live . . . but not this
forever.*

*I step out into the moist, moldy fragrance
of a summer morning and arm in arm with
my enjoyment comes the realization that
never again will he smell this.*

One small misstep and now this neverness.

Nicholas Wolterstorff
from <u>Lament For A Son</u>

CHAPTER 4: ANGER & DENIAL

ANGER

In January of 1994 I started attending meetings of The Compassionate Friends (TCF) regularly. Though I didn't know it at the time, there were no "professional" counselors at these meetings. The "facilitators" who ran the group were all volunteers—all of whom started off as newly grieving parents. During the course of many months I began to tell my story to those who were there to tell theirs. No one there gave me any advice or offered any judgment about what I was describing. Rather, I discovered that emotions I was feeling were not unique to me. All of us at TCF shared these shattered moments.

We talked freely about our lost children and I came to know the children of my new friends as if they were living and breathing. In time I discovered that the loss of every child weighs just the same. No one loss is greater than any other, whether the child was a baby, a youngster, young adult or grown up at the time of his or her death. I eventually determined that the only loss greater than losing a child is to lose two . . . or three.

The anger that began to manifest itself in me was common among every parent I met. Anger at those who avoided the subject of Peter's death for fear of my "uncontrollable" response. Anger at those who couldn't possibly understand what I was feeling. Anger at my own inability to make them understand. Anger at my own thoughts about what might make them understand (and my secret hope that someday they would). The anger at not being understood, at being pitied, at not being pitied, at being singled out, at being given advice. The anger about being told when it was "time" to "feel better," "move on," "get over it," "get on with your life." Anger compounded by not having our children anymore while getting advice from the uninitiated.

During all those meetings I began to talk frankly about how angry everything made me feel. Why was my son singled out, I wondered. Why, among all the people I knew, was I the only one to suffer such a fate. The lack of any rhyme or reason further fueled my anger. It was only during all those meetings at TCF that I could talk openly about how livid everything and everyone made me feel.

The simplest comments enraged me. Once, sitting on a bus, the woman next to me engaged me in conversation. It was very pleasant since we were both going to the same resort area and were sharing some of our local restaurant experiences. It wasn't long before the conversation turned personal, and I realized I was trapped on a bus and couldn't avoid the impending query. And then, there it was. "Do you have children?" she innocently asked me. Responses scrambled around in my brain. I really didn't want to get into the details. I couldn't say no. Then I thought, what if I desperately had wanted children and couldn't have them. Wouldn't that question have caused me a whole set of different painful responses? Suddenly the question, asked by me hundred of times in my own life (and which I most likely had asked strangers over the years), seemed too personal and out of place.

But I had no place to go with my answer. I knew I no longer wanted to maintain the conversation. "I had one." I replied. "Oh," she said, her face darkening. "I'm so sorry." The conversation ended there. It had no place to go. We sat in companionable silence for the rest of the journey, all the while my anger simmering just below the surface.

SORE LOSERS
Spring 2001

It is very hard, if not altogether impossible, to accept the death of one's child with grace. Now, as another season of rebirth and renewal springs forth, I find myself once again, having to swallow an underlying bitterness that I manage, with some difficulty, to keep under cover most of the year.

Spring is here once again. Trees are bursting, flowers are sprouting, children are outside playing and love is blooming. It is a truly irresistible time of year.

And yet, despite my love of the garden and the weather and the magic of nature, I feel an unmistakable sense of anger for all that my child is missing and the joy his loss has robbed me of feeling. Loss like ours, makes us angry. My anger is one thing I cannot and will not relinquish. I carry it as an internal torch that alternately flares and dims with each season, each memorable date, each cataclysmic event reported in the news, every careless comment, every celebration.

Losing this big leaves an unrelenting wound on the soul. Though time may have passed and the sting may have eased, special times cause the anger to bubble up just under the skin. Once there, it doesn't take much to wrench us back into that momentary despair. Spring can do that, including as it does, Mother's Day and Father's Day. Then again, time has also worked for me. It has taught me to understand my anger, to keep it whole but in its place and, even while holding on to it, live my life as fully as possible. I've learned to contain my anger, acknowledge it, take it out now and then and put it away most of the time. Situations and people who cannot help but arouse unwelcome emotion, be they friends, acquaintances or family, are avoided whenever possible.

Enjoying what I have, rather than focusing on all I've lost has become my goal. And having had Peter, such an unmitigated joy in my life, knowing he was mine, understanding finally the impact he has had on me, in making me who I am today, is an amazing realization. For every day I live now, I live to the max . . . for me and for him. Every sunset, every snowfall, every book, every movie, every flower, every little living thing delights me . . . a delight that is more intense for having had the miracle that was Peter in my life and for having had to deal with his leaving.

And though a loss of such magnitude leaves the soul sore for all of time, knowing how much there is to lose makes everything we have left so much more precious.

Treasure the time. We'll all be together again.

NO GREATER PAIN

I know you mean well
But you don't understand
There are no words to explain.
Although on the surface, I may appear fine,
Remember I buried a child of mine
And there is no greater pain.

Grief is a taboo in our civilized world,
I despise this hideous game,
I must smile while going insane.
For Gods' sake, a part of me died,
You can't imagine how often I've cried,
And there is no greater pain.

If I look well,
Or laugh when you joke,
You think I'm my old self again.
I'm raw inside, a shell of me,
The woman you knew can no longer be,
And there is no greater pain.

Look deep in my eyes,
Acknowledge my loss,
As my heart beats its hollow refrain.
I'm caught in a web of infinite whys,
I'll mourn for my son 'till the rest of me dies,
And there is no greater pain.

Madelaine Perri Kasden
Written In Loving Memory of Her Son,
Neill Perri, 10/2/71-6/15/95

THE DUMB REMARK
(or Learning to Forgive the Dumb Remark)
Fall 1998

"Hey, you sound better!"

I stiffen. "Better?"

"Yeah, better." Pause.

"Better than what?" I know just what he means, but as my rage grows, I'm not about to let him off easy.

I was dumbstruck then . . . literally struck dumb. What could I say? I'm talking to a relative who is 3000 miles away. We last saw each other the day Peter died and have spoken only occasionally. Three weeks earlier, the same brilliant comment comes to me from this man's daughter-in-law who has just given birth to her first child . . . his grandchild. With considerable difficulty I am congratulating them and wishing them a lifetime of joy and happiness and each time I elicit the same comment . . . "Hey, you sound better!"

"Better?" I had repeated to her. "I wasn't sick," I had said.

"Well," she continued, "Better than you did a few years ago." We hadn't seen each other or spoken since her wedding day.

What could I say now. He was trapped and I wasn't going to let him get away with it. He should have been wiser than his daughter-in-law. He had suffered loss in his life. He should have known better. "Better?" I went on. "You mean better than when my son died?"

"Yes" he said sheepishly, "Better than when your son died. You sound like you're getting on with your life".

Now I ask you, what could I possibly say? As I write this I am two weeks away from Peter's 5th anniversary. As inconceivable as that is, it is a daily marvel to me that I even wake up every day let alone get on with my life . . . but I do. As you and I know, we have no choice. We know that as dead as we may feel inside, life still beckons. There is no getting away from it.

But now, five years later, the remark brings me back to the beginning. That incredible phone call. Visiting my family in California, it was this relative that took the call from my poor husband—alone in New York when the police came to the door. Enduring all that terror and then having to call me and tell me.

I remember every moment of those first hours in lurid detail. Walking to the phone, my husband telling me there had been an accident, him pleading with me to be brave as I demanded impatiently that he tell me how Peter was. Finally those words, "He died instantly".

The screams haunt me even now as I write. The splitting of my mind as I rose higher and higher away from the moment, looking down at a woman gone mad screaming and flailing wildly on the floor—smashing her head repeatedly on the floor in a desperate attempt to flee an unacceptable reality. And my family struggling to contain the madness. I screamed until my vocal chords gave out and then I screamed without sound. And all the time my husband held the phone in New York—listening and wondering if he was going to lose me too.

It's been quite a journey these past five years. Now, my family, safely 3000 miles away from me, say I sound better. No doubt about it. I'm not screaming anymore. At least no one can hear. I work, I write, I garden. I try to be there for those who are still screaming. And I suppose, to some, I seem quite normal (or read, "over it"). But you and I know the truth.

I am terminally bereaved. My beautiful, smart, funny best friend and son, Peter, is not here loving me unconditionally and forgiving me all my insufficiencies. As the world and the rest of my "family" go about their lives . . . having weddings and birthdays and grandchildren (and comfort themselves because I am not screaming anymore so I must be over it), I live with chronic confusion. A sunny day is beautiful once again, another stray cat can still delight me, watching the garden grow brings a smile to my heart, buying presents for my friends children fills me with anticipation of their delight.

And at the end of each day as I think about what Peter would be doing, I am brought back to the beginning—the phone call . . . the words . . . the screams. And I feel as if it were yesterday and I cry myself to sleep . . . again.

So what can we say to the perpetually ignorant? We are

caught between not wanting to be pitied while insisting that our tragic circumstances and our lost children are never forgotten. I suspect, after five years, that hoping people will someday understand, and stop saying stupid things is an exercise in futility. We have as much chance of ending the dumb remark as we have of ever seeing our kids again.

DENIAL

At our monthly meetings of The Compassionate Friends, every time I told my story, I was met with someone who seemed to be having an identical experience. I began to understand that while each of us grieves uniquely and alone, so much of what we feel has been experienced before—and will surely be experienced again and again. And I, who have become so intimate with death that I can identify with all those who have gone before me and have come after me, still cannot imagine what it must be like to live this experience more than once. If I cannot imagine that, how can someone who has not known such devastation even once, presume to offer any of us advice on how to cope?

SUSPENDING BELIEF
Spring/Summer 1998

As I write this, it is a cold, rainy, windy day, one of the last of the winter of '98. You wouldn't think looking out at the day that today is the first day of Spring and all that it portends. For most of us, and me too, on certain days, the advent of Spring brings on an uplift of spirit at the prospect of rebirth. But for many of us, especially me on certain days, it brings back the reality of my days and the endless sense of disbelief.

This summer will mark the fifth year since our son Peter has called. Unbelievable. I still wait for the phone to ring. It is especially difficult on Friday nights. He always called from school on Friday nights. He knew we would be out at our country house and in for the evening. A few times during these past few years we have gotten a stray call from a telemarketer or an acquaintance on a Friday night. My mind plays tricks on me when the phone rings, and for a millisecond I have to remember. It still happens, even now, almost five years later.

I live all my days in a constant state of disbelief. Some call it denial. What's to accept? Like everyone else at my office, my desk is adorned with my pictures of my handsome son. In the beginning, when I first went back to work at this (then) new job, I was put off by all the young women with young children, always sharing stories with each other, their desks adorned with photos, My response whenever such a conversation began was to flee, to remove myself so as not to be confronted with any questions. After a time I got up the courage to share my situation with my co-workers. Once I had done that I joined their ranks and decorated my desk and wall. From there it was a short step to daily denial. Seeing my son's pictures all day is a tremendous comfort to me. I manage to invent all sorts of scenarios imagining what he might be doing at any given moment. And I talk to his pictures. They are such company.

But I am brought back to my reality weekly. Though

I spend my days in often blissful disbelief, on Friday nights my husband Phil and I have our own little ritual. Though we have Peter's pictures prominently displayed throughout the house, along one wall in the living room is a long bookcase four feet high. Across the top are seven dramatically framed photos of the three of us. In the center, on a handsome brass stand, is Peter's graduation picture taken a few months before he died. I remember when the proofs came to the house. I remember opening the envelope and gasping at how handsome he was, and beginning to cry with disbelief because I couldn't believe he was ours. Now I cry because he wasn't ours long enough.

Now, on Friday nights, when we've settled into the house after the long ride out, we place a 24-hour memory candle beside Peter's picture, we light it and we cry. It is at that moment every Friday that I am forced to suspend my disbelief. I look at those pictures and I rail at the fates, the heavens and all that is holy. I beg and plead and ask all the unanswerable questions. I feel a palpable agony of loss and despair and Phil and I cling to each other and cry . . . and then, when we're cried out for the thousandth time, we move slowly, tentatively back into our reality of suspended belief. Miraculously, the candle burns through Sunday.

Peter was our only child. We have no other children to distract us from our grief. No family surrounds us and forces us to focus on a future. We cling only to each other, adrift together with only a past and a present. Our "somedays" are too scary to contemplate. We plan our future carefully, with the knowledge that there will be no one to care for us in our old age, no one to weep for us when we are gone, no one to light a candle in our memory. Who but our Compassionate Friends could ever comprehend the magnitude of such unbelievable loss?

Despite it all, on any given day you'll call and get my cheery hello, my undaunted sense of humor always at the ready, my positive attitude seemingly intact and my glass always half full—I offer you suspended belief as a tremendous antidote for pain of the soul.

Strange as it seems, as time went on, my anger actually began to comfort me. I could rage inwardly at the ignorance of the unscathed. News commentators were particular targets of mine. As any holiday approached, I was horrified for all the grieving parents who were having joy and happiness rubbed in their faces at every turn. I blamed the media.

God also became a particular target. Every rescued survivor who thanked God on the local or national news received my harangue. Victims of natural disasters, attributing their survival to God's intervention, couldn't hear me railing at their pathetic entreaties to a superpower who I saw as responsible for killing my son and the children of all my new friends as for saving others. God's will took on a whole new meaning. It was my husband, Phil, whose observation that we lived in a world of random chaos, who finally convinced me my battle with God was one I couldn't win.

DISAPPOINTMENTS & SECONDARY LOSSES

Throughout 1994 I took stock of my life. I was fairly sure my time was limited and believed that I would eventually die from my broken heart. There didn't seem to be much reason to go on.

I had always hoped that my own life would serve some higher purpose. A book, a painting—something that would remain even after I was gone. Peter, as it turned out, was my greatest achievement. When nothing earthshaking ever resulted from my efforts, I took comfort in knowing that my son Peter would certainly make his mark upon the world. With Peter dead, Phil and I came face to face with our mortality at very close range, and the realization that nothing lasting would ever result from our having lived at all.

I lost all interest in doing anything. Our house in the country, acquired just days before we discovered I was pregnant with Peter, had been our little haven where, for Peter's entire life, we enjoyed being together. For years we had fixed it up, always in the knowledge that Peter would one day inherit it. Now it too seemed to have no future.

As the months went on, certain friends decided that they couldn't deal with my loss and how I was dealing with it, and disappeared out of my life. Worst of all, my sister and her family in California, after coming east to share my first childless Thanksgiving in 1993, went about their lives after that, with what I felt was barely a thought of me or Peter. My sister, who for twenty years had called me every week before Peter died, called me less and less often. And instead of asking her why, I was too damaged to confront her. I found it easier to nurture my anger and disappointment than to let her know how hurt I was.

As the first anniversary of Peter's death approached, my sister cheerily informed me on the phone that she and her husband were going on a cruise with some friends. We had always vacationed together. Now it seemed, even my family couldn't deal with the reality of my life.

I was devastated. I couldn't believe she wasn't coming to share such a difficult time with me. Realizing how little she thought of the event, too hurt by her lack of concern for me, I couldn't bring myself to ask about her seeming nonchalance about my despair. For years and years afterwards, we grew further and further apart, she feeling she had done all that she could for me, me feeling that she, like many "friends" and acquaintances, had abandoned me. She was my sister. Now, I had lost her too.

Genesse Gentry, a prolific poet after her beautiful daughter Lisa was killed at the age of 18, wrote about these secondary losses that so many bereaved families must incorporate into their lives:

SECONDARY LOSSES

Secondary losses exacerbate the pain
When our children die, leave us adrift,
Struggling to stay sane.

Secondary losses—the world, as a safe place
Where they would thrive, we'd watch them grow,
Now fearful, desolate.

Secondary losses—a friend (or friends) shut off,
Can't look at death this closely—
The fear is tempest tossed.

Secondary losses—the ability to cope
With anything and everything
In a world deprived of hope.

FIRST YOU DIE

Secondary losses—the good things that we held
Have lost all their importance
When misery shrouds our cells.

Secondary losses—our laughter, free from care.
The times we see its reason,
Delightful, now so rare.

Secondary losses—the ability to deny
That terrible things do happen—
Invulnerability, a lie.

Secondary losses—the self confidence we knew,
Our world view so shattered,
Can any part be true?

Secondary losses—the lovely lives we had.
The sunshine that could fill our days,
When rarely we were sad.

Secondary losses, May, transformed, in time come back.
But our children aren't returning.
Nothing, no one, can change that.

Genesse Gentry, *from her book,*
Stars in the Deepest Night, written
In loving memory of her daughter
Lori Ann Elizabeth Gentry,
2/2/70—6/28/91

FLASHBACK
Summer 1999

There was a time when I harbored a secret wish that everyone, for just one brief millisecond, could really know this pain. Then, I would quickly shake off the thought. The terror of what it would mean for anyone else to feel this unmitigated agony brought me back from this fantasy to dealing with what has become, for me, an ongoing reality.

As I write, the television reports unceasingly of the massacre of teen age children at a school in Colorado. My tears and pain for those newly dumbstruck families is so real, I am brought back once more to my own initiation. And now, as this fourth school place disaster strikes, I am beginning to feel more and more, that people may be just beginning to understand the terror . . . that it can happen to you. Things don't just happen to "Other People" anymore. They happen to you.

I am riveted by the images that are replayed over and over. With each repeat image I become so familiar with these new members of our ranks, I begin to think I recognize them. Then slowly, it dawns on me. I am watching myself. I am watching my friends. I recognize all the sounds all the expressions, the body language, the words. "Why?" They keep asking. "Why?" And if they actually came up with an answer . . . would it be enough?

Life as a bereaved parent is a brutal, ongoing, never-ending assault on the senses. The experience, that starts off as a seeming splitting of the mind and escalates into an absolute out-of-body experience, becomes, in time, a permanent, inescapable personality characteristic. It is what gives us a new perspective and sets us on somewhat higher ground. From where we are we sort of look back and down towards the innocent behind us. So many of life's little crises can be placated by the soothing words of a bereaved parent. We know what's really important.

And then, a monstrous event like kids killing kids in another high school in another town. And it all comes rushing back. No perspective here. It is now all over again. The strangled cries of a mother as her mind splits in two. The cracked voice of a father, trying vainly to hold it all together. The dumbstruck sisters and brothers, uncomprehending, reaching out to helpless parents for reassurance that never comes. The friends and relatives trying desperately to make some sense out of a lurid fantasy that will be forever imprinted on the minds and psyches of the survivors. Flashback.

Recently someone said to me, as a statement of fact, "Well surely you don't still think of Peter every minute. It must be somewhat easier now." Oh really? Is that what you think. At night, when you get into bed, just before you close your eyes, do you see what I see? Flashback.

Does the fact that I can be distracted from my reality for several hours each day constitute a cure. That I can laugh at a good story, enjoy a party and dance like no one's watching, mean that I no longer mourn? Flashback. No matter how far we have come, it is always just around the bend. Another flashback.

In three weeks it will be Mother's Day, and a month after that Father's Day—days that have come to mean Survival Day to me. This year, for the newly bereaved parents and siblings of Colorado, Mother's Day and Father's Day comes hard on the heels of their tragedy. In time, they will begin to learn the special coping skills that are needed in this alien place. To most parents, Mother's Day celebrates the daily survival of modern parenthood—clothing, feeding, nurturing, chauffeuring, teaching, scheduling, juggling, loving, supporting—all while putting up with the pressures of balancing job and home.

But we have come to a different kind of celebration. I call it Survivor Mother's Day and Father's Day. For the day commemorates for us, a special kind of heroics—not for having survived—for we all know you don't die from this—but for having survived so well. For taking the cloak of grief and hanging it away during the day so we can appear whole to the rest of the world—taking it out during our alone or special times . . . like flashbacks. For re-engaging in life despite an invisible burden that lurks just under the skin—ready to erupt just when we think we have it all together . . . another flashback. For recognizing that only our survival assures the memory of our lost children. And for bearing the unbearable, again and again, through every flashback.

CHAPTER 5: SURVIVING THE HOLIDAYS

OLYMPICS OF THE SOUL
Fall 2000

These are the last few days of summer. Soon the leaves will turn and fall, the days will grow mercifully shorter, the temperature will drop and we will retreat to the safe comfort of home. For just a brief period, we can watch the world from the safety of the nest, not enticed out into the games of summer by well meaning friends and family, intent on our participation. We need this time to prepare . . . to prepare for the next Olympics of the soul . . . the Holidays.

Much has been written about getting through the holidays when you are grieving. The intensity of the pain of the recently bereaved, the suggestions of how to manage by the experienced griever, the wistful thoughts of the poets . . . so much to be said about this particular period of survival. Truth is, for me the holidays are only a tad more difficult than every other day. Like salt in a wound, the over-the-top joyousness adds an extra dose of emotional pain. But I've come to realize that many who "celebrate" the holidays are also fellow travelers along this grieving path. They're just further ahead than many of us are. I'm still not up to the festivities. For me, it remains a time of introspection. With absolutely no opportunity to mourn our losses at this time of year, I choose to remain as low key as possible, and venture back into the ebb and flow of days only after New Year's Eve.

It's not possible for the uninitiated to comprehend the emotional roller coaster we are on now. But I recently came across a column written, appropriately, by an Australian mom. Though not written with the holidays in mind, for me it expresses the way I spend much of my time during this particular season. With the Olympics recently completed there, I wanted to share it with you:

IF ONLY THEY KNEW ...
By Jan McNess, TCF, Victoria, Australia

If only they knew when I speak of him, I am not being morbid, I am not denying his death. I am proclaiming his life. I am learning to live with his absence. For 26 years he was a part of my life, born, nurtured, molded and loved; this cannot be put aside to please those who are uncomfortable with my grief.

If only they knew that when I sit quietly, apparently content with my own company, I am not self indulgently unhappy, dwelling on things which cannot be changed; I am with him, I am seeing his face, hearing his voice, remembering his laughter, recalling his excitement and joy in life. Please allow me this time with him as I do not begrudge you your time with your children.

If only they knew when I sometimes weep quietly, I do not cry in self-pity for what I have lost. I weep for what he has lost; for the life he loved, for the music which filled his very being and for all he still longed to hear, for the poetry which moved him to tears, for the beauty about him that daily fed his soul, for the exhilaration and excitement of flying the skies, of searching for his God in the vast space of the universe. For all that he loved and lost, I cry.

If only they knew the feeling of deep grief, the emptiness and dull pain, the endlessness of death. If only they understood the insanity of the platitudes so freely spoken; that "time heals," that "you'll get over it," that "it was for the best," that "God takes only the best", and realize that these are more an insult than a comfort, that the warm and compassionate touch of another means so much more.

If only they knew that we will not find true peace and tranquility until we are prepared to try to stand in the shoes of others. We will not be understood until we learn to understand compassionately and we will not be heard until we learn to listen with our hearts as well as our minds.

As this Holiday season begins, I pray that we all find it in our hearts and minds to be thankful for what we have and grateful for having had what we've lost.

FIRST THANKSGIVING

For the first six months after Peter died I stayed home. As luck would have it, the company I had been working for conveniently went out of business, so I wasn't under any pressure to go back to work. The truth was that I didn't really think I could or would ever work again. I began waiting for death to overtake me and spent most of my time crying, and trying to become familiar with what I would find in the next world. I wrote a will and began to divest myself of some of my more treasured possessions. As Thanksgiving approached, I thought it would be a good idea for my sister, her husband and their son and daughter to come east (from California) to visit. I hoped it would be a diversion from what had always been my favorite holiday, which I now dreaded.

Unfortunately, the presence of my family—on the East coast for the first time in 22 years—only served to underscore the absence of Peter. It was a painful miscalculation on my part. Although the holiday served my initial intention, it was so total a diversion that it literally eliminated the loss of Peter as a possible subject of conversation. There was no talking about Peter (and bemoaning life without him), and I discovered that I needed to talk about him.

Somehow, talking about him helped keep his memory alive and vibrant. Sadly, talking about our children often makes folks who have not experienced this devastating loss uncomfortable. Yet, for many bereaved parents, the more we can talk about our children, the better we feel. No doubt this is one of the primary reasons we find comfort at meetings of The Compassionate Friends.

Conversely, knowing how uncomfortable our losses make the uninitiated feel, when we do run into them we find ourselves almost apologizing for having to "break the news" about our loss. Alone again after my family's return home to California, I began to avoid the possibility of meeting anyone who did not know that Peter had died. At the holidays, when I received cards from distant old friends and acquaintances, I responded without telling them what had happened. Seeing neighbors in the street who didn't yet know about Peter, I would turn to avoid a chance meeting that would obligate me to tell them. In this way, I felt that they would maintain the thought of a living, breathing Peter. Introduced to people for the first time, if I sensed the conversation might lead to the question of children, I would work diligently to steer the conversation elsewhere.

I realize that this contradicted my very strong need to talk about Peter, but complicated, confusing thoughts became the order of the day. I thought that Peter being dead, and Phil and I being bereaved parents, might, in some way, cause people to judge us. Sadly, I wasn't too far off the mark. How many times has a bereaved mother been hailed a hero for just surviving? How many times have we been told, "if it was me I would die!" It's as if surviving indicates you loved your child less—so obviously untrue.

Consequently, fearing being judged on my behavior while grieving, not revealing my story became my method of choice. I may have been projecting my own responses, but I didn't care. I knew whenever I descended in the elevator of my apartment building, that neighbors of a nodding acquaintance would smile gently, making me feel an object of their pity. They felt sorry for me. I was beginning to understand the humiliation Phil talked about feeling when he got back to work. I also knew that based on my appearance, and its semblance of well-being, that I looked like I was "getting over it"—something which is never to be the case.

THE WAY WE WERE
Fall 1997

The "Holiday" season comes barreling towards us like a runaway train. Contemplating an appropriate topic for this column, and trying to avoid the obvious, I find that the "Holidays" just won't stay down. I have no soothing platitudes to help us get through the coming weeks. As my fifth Thanksgiving without Peter looms, I am possessed by thoughts of how very different my life has become. Perhaps some of you can identify with these gleanings of happier times.

I used to look forward to the season. Though Christmas isn't my holiday, one cannot help (especially if you live in New York City) getting caught up in it. Besides being so pretty, there is an epidemic of almost tangible energy throughout the season that is unavoidably contagious. Everything is magnified. The colors, the lights, the music, the joy. And now, the sadness. I used to look forward to the season. Now I look back.

It begins in mid-November when cooking and menu planning begin, weeks before Thanksgiving. Among civilians, there is the heightened sense of happy anticipation; travel plans being made; talk of family and friends being together. Then, the fond wishes to co-workers on the eve of everyone's departure to their turkey destination . . . the laughs, the pictures to be taken, the memories to be born, the partying, the revelry.

Now I am painfully aware of how quiet it all has become.

There is no more family for me. I keep a low profile as those around me share stories, recipes and plans. On Thanksgiving Day, my husband and I will share the smallest turkey I can possibly find. We will spend the day quietly and alone, candles burning in memory, while we reflect with dismay on how quickly it all ended for us.

Oh, don't get me wrong. We tried that first Thanksgiving to remain a part of it all. My sister, her husband, and her two grown children went to great effort and expense to come to New York and try to replicate a "family" holiday. But coming from California and North Carolina, it was the first and only time we had ever been together for Thanksgiving. And, with my nephew in school, they had all been apart for months so it was quite a reunion for them. It shouldn't have surprised me that their presence only served to magnify the absence of Peter. Naturally, they never got it. To this day, I am sure they all believe they did everything they could to be some comfort. The weekend remains a bitter memory for me—especially now—when years later we hardly ever speak. It's probably not that my family is any different. It is that I am so changed.

More than four years later, we've decided it's better for us now to stay softly, gently in the background and reflect on what we did have. We did, after all, have so much.

It gets easier after Thanksgiving. Thanksgiving remains the point of entry to the "holiday season." With all its memories, it has become a painful rite of passage into the most relentlessly joyous time of the year. By Christmas, the activity takes on a life of its own. It becomes so frenetic there is hardly time to be sad about what we have become. I can get caught up in the manic hysteria without being emotionally involved. I can buy a few impersonal gifts; stuff envelopes with cash to thank the many people who service our lives; go to a few office parties, and have a few laughs without batting an eye.

No. On reflection, it's Thanksgiving that gives me the greatest pause. Because Thanksgiving is that once-a-year day that really underscores the past, and exposes me as the changed, vulnerable person I've become. Thanksgiving, when I must be thankful for everything I had and everything we were.

It's interesting to reflect on how the holidays continue to affect us even through the passing years. While those around us barely give a thought to the continuing turmoil inside, we always know that, despite appearances, time only helps us to compartmentalize our sensitivity. The good news is that learning how to maneuver through the landscape ultimately allows us to begin to let a little joy creep back into our lives.

THE END OF THE 20TH CENTURY

As 1999 was winding down, and the Millennium approached, a particularly heavy case of melancholy descended on me. The anticipated celebrations brought forth a relentless cascade of references to great hopes for the future, and peace for all mankind. The impending joyousness was almost too much to bear.

I was left out of it, watching the celebrants from my "alien" perspective. The preceding century—and the past seven years without Peter—had been enough to convince me that the future would never meet their expectations. "Happy New Year" continued to have a hollow ring.

THE MILLENNIUM IS COMING!
Holiday 1999

The Millennium is coming! The Millennium is coming! A cry is heard throughout the land!

It seems to me that the crescendo of Millennium madness has been in the air and building all my life. Though I've lived almost my whole life in the second half of the century, my consciousness seems to have put the turn of the last century into long past history, and the turn of the next way off into some distant future. Now that the century's end is being counted down in double digits, I find myself thinking of where I've been . . . and where I might be going.

I remember when Peter was small and we talked about how old he would be at the turn of the century. He would be 28 . . . almost 30. I would be . . . The thought of how old I would be usually served to change my thought process. Now I ruminate on the time like an old crone in a home. The future has no shape, only the past.

As youngsters we always made a big deal out of New Year's Eve. What we were planning to do began to take on major importance around Thanksgiving. Once plans were set, and partying was the rule, we set out in earnest to dance and play and celebrate all the promise of a new year. We rang out the old and rang in the new. As Peter grew older, he too began to plan each New Year celebration, months in advance, as I had.

I don't know when the changing of the year began to drift into my consciousness with a small sense of impending dread. When did I begin to think it might be more fun to stay home and celebrate quietly? Was it after a friend drove off a country road into a tree after a party? Was it when I knew Peter was going out with friends and I wanted to be home, waiting? Was it after my Dad died, or my Mom? Was it when my friends, many of whom are considerably older, began to leave this world? Was it when Peter died?

Now, with the approaching Millennium, and the seeming need so many have to ring out this century and ring in the next with some particularly over-the-top celebration, I find myself retreating even more into a quiet, pensive, reflective sense of mind. I feel as though I can see the future, and it scares me. This is the century I know. This is territory that is familiar. I've been here. I can do this.

And then, there is all I leave behind. My history. My past. Some friends. My parents. My son.

When that bell rings and that ball drops on December 31, 1999, we all step over into uncharted territory. Or do we? Will there be no war, no illness, and no natural disasters? Will it be a century in which children will no longer die? With all that we now know about life, can we look forward to a relief from our pain? No, I'm afraid that for all the newness and excitement that the new century holds for those with less experience, those of us who have feasted at this buffet called life, who have tasted real joy and known extraordinary pain, will look at this crossing as one to be taken quietly and with considerable introspection.

As we move ahead into this new century I, for one, will still be taking it one day at a time. I will continue to fill each day with as much activity as I can squeeze into 24 hours. I will continue to learn how to navigate my way through an electronic world that didn't exist just a few years ago . . . a world my precious son never got to know. And I will become really knowledgeable about all the new things there are to learn so that I can tell funny and amusing stories and anecdotes about my later life. Because there is one thing I do know about the next century.

In the next century I'll be reunited with Peter. And we'll sit across from one another telling each other stories, making each other laugh, safe at last in the knowledge that we are together again.

CHAPTER 6: THE SPIRITUAL SIDE

LOOK TO THE STARS

I look to the stars and I see you there.
It may seem that all that can be known
Of your life is a quick flash, just a small
Part of the excitement and the confusion,
The certainty and the doubt that once was
You.

But I know more. I know that bravest part
Of you, the part that risked loving. So when
I look up to see you, I have no doubt that
At least your courage will shine forever.

Molly Fumia, <u>Safe Passage</u>

I was home during the months following Peter's death and the winter of 1994 was particularly harsh. I remember looking out the window as storm after storm ravaged the city, content that the weather seemed to match the chill that had settled on my soul. Only with the advent of Spring did I begin to despair at the prospect of renewal. I had begun to explore the possibility of an ongoing existence beyond life as we know it. I read book after book that confidently exclaimed the absolute existence of an afterlife. Witness after witness expounded on messages from their lost ones that "proved" that when we left the physical body, our soul continued on apace, having learned the lessons that our brief time here in earth's laboratory was meant to teach.

As you can imagine, the idea that Peter might have simply ceased to exist became harder and harder to accept. A recently bereaved sibling gave me a book written by a "psychic medium" who claimed to talk to dead people. My first reaction was to toss the book, but the temptation to read it was too great. I opened it and began what has become an ongoing search for evidence of a spiritual afterlife.

One morning, while the TV played "The Joan Rivers Show," I was moving from room to room at home when a young man who claimed to be one of these psychic mediums came on as a guest. Both my husband Phil and I were drawn to the set, and we avidly listened to the interview and demonstration. Several people from the audience were chosen as subjects. We were riveted as the young psychic revealed significant clues about the dead relatives of the participants. I began to fantasize about someone being able to communicate with Peter. Peter had such a powerful presence that, certainly, if there was "another side," he was definitely capable of making his presence felt.

At a Compassionate Friends meeting the following month I overheard a conversation regarding James Van Praagh, the medium we had seen on "The Joan Rivers Show." Van Praagh was coming to New York and one member of the group, who had "discovered" him a few years earlier, had agreed to help him find a place to do a demonstration. I wheedled myself into the conversation, volunteering to help find a venue.

My offer was happily accepted and Van Praagh contacted me by telephone a week later. We liked each other immediately. He explained the type of space he was looking for and I began my search. He would be in New York in July, a month before the first anniversary of Peter's death. In exchange for my efforts on his behalf, he agreed to give me a private reading.

My experience of that reading was stunning, to say the least. James brought forth so much evidence of Peter's continuing existence and love that I arrived home in a state of euphoria. I had no doubt that I had been with Peter during the reading. There were so many little things that had happened through the year since Peter's death—which Van Praagh made reference to—things that were just too coincidental. At last, here was James Van Praagh confirming that the soul continues. And not just anyone's soul—Peter's soul! I didn't trust my memory. I took out my journal and wrote a letter to Peter. I thanked him for all his reassurances, and poked some fun at his new method of communication.

By now I was calling Van Praagh James, and we became

great friends. Eventually, because of time constraints, he stopped giving private readings but continued to give demonstrations in cities around the country. Whenever he came to New York I would arrange for a small group of my interested "compassionate friends" to have their own demonstration.

One stormy night, with thunder and lightening raging outside a Manhattan hotel, James wowed 40 of my friends, as messages from their children, their mothers and fathers, and a host of friends and relatives, poured in from the spiritual world. Even I wasn't exempt. A message from my mother, as well as one from Peter, came through that night. I remember thinking then, and continue to wonder, why skeptics work so hard to debunk the believers among us. The comfort and peace that comes with such messages, however fleeting, cannot be measured. The next morning, walking uptown, I thought again about the dynamic between believers and skeptics. Who wins as each side strives to make its point?

ON CHOICES, CRUSADES, GOD,
. . . and other questions
Summer 1997

Walking to work on a bright and breezy Spring morning, these are the words that keep going through my head. The night before, during a violent thunderstorm, I had been witness to an extraordinary event with my friend James Van Praagh, the well-known psychic medium. The day was crystal clear, and my emotional responses to the previous evening kept bringing me back to all the people I have met during the past few years who insist on denying any possibility of a spiritual existence. Why do they do that? How do they know?

As a child, I can remember one of my favorite TV shows. It was called "Topper," and it was all about "ghosts" named George and Marion, who had perished in a car accident. Friends of Cosmo Topper, George, Marion, and their dog, inhabited Topper's house but remained invisible to everyone save Cosmo Topper. This led to an ever on-going series of improbable, often hilarious, occurrences, and formed my mental image of what it must be like to be dead. As a child, it seemed to be somewhat amusing. More recently, the movie "Ghost" served to further feed my fantasy . . . to believe that there is something beyond this life—and entertaining once again. But when we lost our son Peter almost four years ago, the last thing I wanted to hear was that, "He was in a better place." The very thought made me cringe and want to strike out at anyone who dared to suggest such a thing. Then someone dropped a book in my bag.

The book was written by a "psychic medium" and after I angrily tossed it aside, something made me ultimately pick it up and begin to read. I became hooked almost at the first sentence. As the author recounted tales of receiving messages from "the other side," and described the evidence that made believers out of skeptics, I began to wonder once more . . . Could it be?

I continued to read. I read book after book, written by highly intelligent people, all of whom passionately believed in the existence of another life . . . a life "in spirit." After a relentless search, I did finally meet with a psychic medium . . . someone who communicates with spirits . . . and was overcome by the evidence he brought of my son's ongoing existence . . . I too decided to believe. It was a choice I made. I chose to believe.

My belief has nothing to do with religion and is in a constant state of flux. It blossoms and fades depending on the day. I want, also, to believe in God. Now, however, I am having some disagreement with God and am hard pressed to believe in anything. But I do hope to make my peace with God someday, and believe once more.

Meanwhile, as others skeptically laugh off my constant search for verification of a spiritual "life," or angrily insist they do not believe and are offended at any discussion around them of the possibilities that some of us hope for . . . I continue.

But I am not on a crusade. I never try to convince a non-believer. My choice is for me. It comforts me. Many bereaved parents find considerable comfort, as I do, in the possibilities . . . I've never met someone on the same quest as mine, who does believe in a spiritual existence, and who tries to convince anyone else to believe. But I have met several who do not believe and who go out of their way to convince those who find comfort in the possibility that their loved ones continue on in spirit, to dash those hopes and destroy what little peace comes along with the dream. Why do they do that?

During my quest, I met and became a good friend of James

Van Praagh. Shortly after Peter died, I had a "reading" with him and was so overwhelmed by the evidence he gave me . . . information he could only have gotten, in my view, from Peter . . . I was euphoric. When I went home that evening, I told my husband I had been with Peter. As I recounted the story, I could tell that even my husband, the skeptic, wanted desperately to believe. I became aware, after that visit, of the many messages (or coincidences) we were getting, I hoped, from Peter.

As time has gone on, I have noticed my belief has dimmed at times. "Messages" seem to have gotten fewer. But I always remember the comfort I got from my friend . . . James Van Praagh. And I have gone on to take great comfort in the moments of peace I have often watched him bring to many of my Compassionate Friends.

Despite those non-believers who look upon us with disdain, I continue to take vicarious pleasure in the comfort I see James bring to other bereaved parents like myself. And on this stormy Spring evening, I invited several of my friends to meet with him in the hope that some would experience some message, some evidence that their own loved one was still present in their lives. And we were all rewarded . . . as unbelievable message after message, including several from Peter . . . were brought into our tragically altered lives. And, for a few brief moments, we all "knew" once again that we would all be reunited someday. Fact or fiction? Does it really matter if it brings even a fragment of momentary relief?

So we have choices. We can choose to find a way to manage

this altered state we find ourselves in. We can chose to believe in more or chose to believe in nothing more. We can share our experience or we can crusade to convince those who believe that there is nothing to believe in. We can be angry with God or accepting of God. Or we can proselytize about our belief or non-belief in God. In this mother's view, it really doesn't matter. As long as we don't inflict more pain. Whatever little comfort we can garner. Whatever works . . . isn't it all okay in the end?

TELLING MY STORY

In the Spring of 2000, James Van Praagh invited me to tell my story in his new book, <u>Healing Grief</u>. I welcomed the opportunity to reflect once again on this incredible journey. Looking back through my early journals, I came upon a letter I wrote to Peter after meeting James for the first time in 1994. The following was published in <u>Healing Grief</u> in 2000. Though some of the following material has appeared elsewhere in this book, I've chosen to leave this chapter intact, as it appeared in Van Praagh's book.

MY ONLY SON

Saturday, August 7, 1993, dawned a seemingly perfect day. Visiting my sister and her family in California, she and I decided it was the perfect day to drive down to Carmel to walk around and do some "sport shopping"—the kind where you look but don't buy. We needed to be back early because my nephew was leaving for graduate school and my niece was throwing him a farewell party.

We left at 9 a.m. and had a predictably perfect day. My son Peter, who had just graduated from Syracuse, was back in New York with my husband, Phil, interviewing for jobs in the music publishing business. I had spoken to him Thursday night after he had completed a second interview with a company he hoped to work for. He was excited and told me in detail everything that was said at the interview. I assured him it was "a lock." I had no doubt he had landed the job.

On Friday night, Peter went out with a few of his college buddies, in town for the weekend. The weather had been terrible all day, so by 10 p.m. boredom had set in and the prospect of barhopping held considerable appeal. It was a bad choice. By 2 a.m. Peter lay dead on a Manhattan highway—killed instantly when the young man who was driving lost control of his speeding car on a rain slicked road, shooting my precious son out the rear window like a rocket. Four boys in a car. Three shaken and bruised. One perfect child—dead in an instant.

Peter was our only child. Unlike the relationship he had with my husband, he and I shared a very special kinship. All mothers love their sons, but there was a unique bond between us that everyone noticed. It was as if we could communicate telepathically—completing each other's thoughts and anticipating each other's needs. Because we were a family of three—there was always that sort of "two against one" dynamic. And since Peter's sense of humor was even fiercer than mine, it was usually the two of us against Phil. Poor Phil never had a chance when Peter and I were "on."

And in my adoring eyes and heart, Peter could do no

wrong. I was putty in his hands from the time he could crawl, and he knew it. What saved me was that he adored me as much as I worshipped him. In his view I was bigger than life. There was nothing—no problem his Mom couldn't solve. Nothing I couldn't do. No quip I couldn't toss back. And I reveled in his hero worship. My life bordered on perfect. You know how it goes. When something seems too good to be true—it usually is.

When my sister and I returned from Carmel that Saturday afternoon we were exhausted. My brother-in-law was waiting and we decided to forego the farewell party, order a pizza and watch a movie. We had just popped the video into the VCR when the phone rang. It was 9 p.m. Midnight in New York. Peter had been dead for 22 hours and I never suspected a thing. It simply wasn't a possibility.

The shock and disbelief of that moment is so indelibly branded on to the surface of my mind, that all succeeding experience has had to work its way through the scar tissue of that injury. This has, as a result, become, to some extent, shaped a different perspective on life and the world as I once knew it. I like to believe that Peter defined who I was. There are many who are quick to argue that this perspective is simply not acceptable.

But, for many of us, especially those who have lost their only child, it is a deep-seeded truth. Don't get me wrong. I have always had a very full life. I've always been in business and, as a result of my affiliations, I've traveled around the world and participated in a life filled with the most accomplished and celebrated people in my industry. My affiliations and associations brought me great personal satisfaction.

Yet with all the glamour and the glory, my greatest joy and satisfaction came in being Pete's Mom. In my view, nurturing this child and accompanying him through life and into manhood was the greatest honor, joy and achievement of my life.

And Peter loved me unconditionally, the way a parent loves a child. This is no small thing. We love our children no matter what. Even an ax murderer's mother can't help loving that child. And children can't help loving their parents. But too often that is a qualified love. Peter and I had a devotion and mutual admiration that defied ordinary description. I've since heard many bereaved parents try to describe this kind of affiliation. Some parent/child relationships have a consistency that transcends simple explanation. Ours was one of these. His now being dead was not only unacceptable and unthinkable, it left me in a world where that particular love and acceptance was now non-existent.

I was alone. Surrounded by disbelieving friends and disconnected family, I was alone in the universe. Only Peter could have imagined my pain. And that thought increased the torment. If there was another side of life, then he knew he had left me here alone and was equally in torment on the other side. In my mind's eye, I saw us both churning in an agony of unrelenting grief.

My Mom died in 1988. She and I had as close a relationship as I had with Peter. She had been failing for several years before she died and indeed, at the end, we had an intense period of several days where we had an opportunity to say many of the things you rarely get to say to someone before they leave this life. Jokingly she told me that if there really is another side, she'd find a way to get a message to me.

Her death left me bereft and I waited for a sign. None ever came. My sister, on the other hand, kept telling me how she felt Mom's presence everywhere. It infuriated me to think that my mother had probably decided to spend her eternity in California. She probably figured she and I had said all there was to say and she was determined to provide my sister with as complete a goodbye as I had. I was disappointed, and just a little bit angry.

Unlike my Mom's death, Peter's death, just five years later, brought me face to face with my own death. Death became my total focus. I needed to know everything about it since I was sure I was dead but my body had not caught up with my mind. The people that mattered to me most in the world were now in another world. I needed to get there quickly. And I needed to study the terrain so that I could navigate the territory and find my way to Peter as quickly as I could.

I began by reading everything I could find about death. As soon as I was left alone, I would venture out to the bookstore. There I would head directly to the section called *"Death & Dying."* I would sit on the floor and begin my research. (The mega-bookstore complete with easy chairs and coffee bars was yet to be invented). I'd start at the top shelf and work my way down—George Anderson to Kubler-Ross. By the end of the day I'd work my way home . . . my mind reeling . . . mostly at my growing belief in the real possibility of a continuum of life . . . that perhaps I should begin my quest in earnest. All that

I was reading seemed to validate my growing belief that Peter, so much larger than life in so many ways, could simply not be over. My quest began.

During the winter of 1994, just six months after Peter died, my husband and I were spending a quiet weekend out on Long Island at our house near the beach. The TV was on and "The Joan Rivers Show" had, as a guest, a young psychic medium who was demonstrating that he could receive messages from "the other side." We sat riveted as several volunteers from the audience had "readings" and appeared to receive messages from their dead children. I knew I had to see this young man. His name was James Van Praagh and, when I looked into his eyes on the screen, I knew I would find him.

Shortly after Peter died, I began going to meetings at an international support group called The Compassionate Friends. This organization, with chapters all around the world, proved to be the lifeline I needed to survive. A few weeks after seeing James on "The Joan Rivers Show," I overheard a conversation at one of our Compassionate Friends meetings. It seemed James was coming to New York, was hoping to give a demonstration and needed some help from one of the members of the group (whom he had befriended) in finding an appropriate space that would hold upwards of 100 people. I immediately volunteered my services. Maybe I could manage to get a private reading with the man who now had become an obsession.

On June 17, 1994, ten months after Peter's sudden death, I finally got my wish. My long awaited private reading with James Van Praagh was scheduled for 7 p.m. That entire day

I was in an intensely heightened state of anticipation. The day seemed endless as I watched the clock and counted the minutes. I felt the way I had as a youngster anticipating my first date. And I knew, as the minutes ticked by, that Peter was as nervous and excited as I was. We both knew we would be together that evening. And we were right.

My visit began promptly at seven. James has a great sense of humor and so do I. Peter also had an irrepressible sense of humor—indeed, my husband always called me his laugh track—he could hardly say hello without making me laugh. His sense of humor was immediately apparent to James. During the course of our two hours together, James and Peter both seemed to be having a wonderful time, sending me message after message, becoming more and more "present" in the process.

By the time our visit ended I felt I had actually spent the evening with Peter. I was elated, and went home giddy with the sense of real connection and knowing that Peter was okay—and knowing that it had been as important for him to connect with me as it was for me to have connected with him. I was convinced. He was okay. He continued. He was somewhere.

When I got home I was more at peace than I had been for ten months. That night, I wrote Peter a letter. It is remarkable to read, even now . . .

Dear Peter:

I went to see James Van Praagh tonight. Because I am always compelled to record my thoughts (all of which, to date, are totally filled with despair), I simply must record some of what transpired and some of what I'm feeling. First of all, and most important, right this minute, I am not overwhelmed with sadness and hopelessness. That in itself astounds me. I also do not feel alone. I am somehow, right this minute, convinced you are here with me. I feel momentarily overcome when I think that I cannot touch you, or hug you or laugh with you or cry with you. But I am comforted to know that you are with me so often.

Yesterday, all day, I felt this delicious anticipation . . . as if I had a date. I felt like I was going to see you and I had the distinct feeling that you were doing the same thing over there . . . even though there is no time there. I felt you almost pacing around waiting for me to finally get to James so we could be together again. Meeting James was wonderful. He's instantly likeable and has an innocence about him that makes him easy to trust. I also felt even more convinced that I was indeed with you again.

As time goes on, and I continue to digest all the evidence, I'm sure I will have many more questions. But what I really wanted last night was evidence . . . a statement from you that you were okay. I felt, going in, that nothing less would do. Even though I had no idea what could possibly transpire that would convince me that your beautiful spirit lives on.

So now I ask; should I be convinced?

Were you there when I folded the blanket and tried to get it to stay up on the top shelf of the closet? Should I be impressed that you knew I was talking to someone about going into the hospital just an *hour before I met with James? That I had thought of calling Isaac on the way to James?*

Did you tell James about the cartons? The ones we had all over the house while we packed to move out for another summer? Did you really watch me wrap and pack all the pictures?

Do you really miss me honey?

I will admit that it was pretty clever of you to tell James about your room . . . that we haven't changed a thing and probably never will. That there's a mirror in your room surrounded by things with words on it . . . your diplomas and fraternity stuff . . . that there's something hanging on the mirror . . . I can't figure it out until I get home and find the tassels from all your graduation caps; Jr. High School, High School and College, hanging on the mirror.

And of course, the pile of magazines . . . in the living room. I should get rid of them you say. And the door that was giving us problems . . . the one that developed a nasty squeak last week that Daddy had to fix? And that wonderful mention of all the things around the house that need fixing—suggesting Daddy get on it? I loved that.

Oh yes. That little mention of Atlantic City. Knowing I was there a short while ago playing the slots . . . and losing. Saying you tried to help but couldn't. You didn't do so well in that department when you were here. What made you think you could help now?

Oh yes. The baseball caps. Telling James about all your caps. And your music. And your pictures on the refrigerator. As you suggested,

I shall place something in the kitchen that makes noise so that you can try to let me know when you are around. And I shall continue to watch for something that you manage to knock off the shelves in the red living room. Nice touch, that clue.

I'm glad you liked the poem I had your friends read at your service. And I'm glad I didn't let Lauren come. You had enough girlfriends and ex-girlfriends at your graveside weeping. My favorite affirmation, though, was that you were indeed at your service at Syracuse. It was an extraordinary day. I had hoped you were there and when I went up to the podium to speak, I thought I saw the air move up in the left balcony. No one was up there . . . but I felt you there.

And then, when the bouquet of roses fell over at the end, after standing there all day, with no one moving, no vibrations . . . and not a slow slipping but a sudden flop . . . as if some unseen hand had simply whacked it over! Well, then I knew. I knew you were there. James got a real kick out of that. Threw in the question about where your picture was too. Not necessary. I got it.

So, my darling, welcome back. In whatever form you take. I'll take whatever I can get until we are together again. Tell Poppa I remember Niagara Falls. I'm so glad you are with Nana.

Sunday is Father's Day. Daddy should be much comforted by your message of love. I know I am.

I don't anticipate any future joy in my life. I will still find myself in the depths of despair most of the time. But, today I feel a strange reassurance that we are not over. And, for that, I thank you and I thank James Van Praagh.

I love you Peter. And I miss you. And I shall try to go on to my natural end with a touch of grace. But I shall spend every day of my life looking forward to the next time we can get together. I can hardly wait.

CHAPTER 7: RE-ENTRY

DID I TEACH YOU TOO WELL ABOUT HEAVEN?

Did I teach you too well about heaven?
Did I make it sound too good?
Were you so very eager to get there,
That you went before you should?

I didn't want you to be afraid,
To be doubtful or unsure.
I described a wonderful heaven to you,
And made you feel secure.

I know you believed unfailingly,
In God and the immortal soul;
In a heaven where loved ones reunite,
Broken families are once again whole.

Did I teach you too well about heaven?
When the angel of death came to call,
You left without struggle or argument;
Without any objection at all.

When you were still a child,
As your mother I assuaged your fears.
I never imagined you'd be so convinced,
Or sacrifice so many years.

If I taught you too well about heaven,
And you willingly entered the light,
I hope heaven is all that I promised.
God, I beg and I pray I was right.

Madelaine Perri Kasden
Written In Loving Memory of Her Son,
Neill Perri, 10/2/71-6/15/95

LITTLE STEPS

A bout eight months after Peter died, a friend called about a temporary consulting job with a bridal company. Acknowledging my lifetime of experience in the fashion industry, everyone, from my husband to my remaining friends, encouraged me to give it a try.

Trying to control my anxiety, I took the job believing I would never be able to manage it. Once I proved how non-functional I was, people would leave me alone to grieve in peace.

Going back to work took superhuman effort. Getting out of bed and getting dressed was hard enough, but actually opening the door and leaving the house was terrifying.

Fear was my constant companion. The impossible—losing Peter—had already happened. If that could happen, so could anything else. Crossing the street, every car looked like it was headed for me. A construction site surely had a brick or a plank or some such contrivance that was designed to fall directly on my head. People walking beside me in the street were undoubtedly targeting me for some sinister mayhem. And my paranoia wasn't only for me. I worried that my husband Phil was vulnerable too. If anything were to happen to him, what would I do?

Despite these unreasonable fears, I did manage to go off to work at the bridal studio. It was located on the second floor of a brownstone on 68th Street—familiar territory for me since I had worked in the neighborhood many years before. Each day as I climbed the steps I would begin thinking about the day's schedule. During the course of the day I was preoccupied with clients, fabrics, appointments, deadlines, financials . . . all the details of running a business. It wasn't until the end of the day, as I descended the stairs to the street, that thoughts of Peter would again fill my mind and the tears would cloud my vision all the way home.

The eight-week consultancy turned into eight months. I discovered that work was therapeutic. All of the skills I had developed in my 20-year career came into play. For several hours each day I was distracted enough to think about business . . . not death. By the end of the year, I told several friends that I would probably be looking for a job after the holidays. "Keep an eye out for a job for me," I said. As it turned out—work could work.

Simultaneously with working, I was getting more involved with the Manhattan Chapter of The Compassionate Friends. Meetings had become a source of strength for me and, as the months passed and newly bereaved parents found their way there, I began to share more of my thoughts with them. It also became apparent to me that those who had recently lost a child were now looking at me as if I were an experienced bereaved parent! *I* was now the source of some hope for survival to them! I was amazed. After all, what answers could *I* possibly provide? In my heart I knew there were no answers. But in the very beginning, you don't want to believe that.

And that's when I knew that dealing with Peter's death was going to be a lifelong journey, one that I would never stop traveling. I realized, too, that each of us would need to learn about whatever little experience others on the path could share. Knowing what might lie ahead would help us to maintain our footing from baby step to baby step. I was also surprised to discover that helping newcomers navigate the terrain added unexpected purpose to my own newly restructured life.

SOME THOUGHTS ON HOPE . . .
Winter 1997

The dictionary defines hope as entertaining a wish for something with some expectation . . . to look forward with confidence . . . that which is desired or anticipated . . .

It is 42 months since our son Peter was killed. At the time I remember thinking, "abandon all hope who enters here." I knew then that I had entered a different place, an uncharted place, a dark place. The only hope I entertained was the hope that I would join Peter sooner rather than later. I became acquainted, even intimate, with despair.

Time after such an event becomes concentrated. So much emotional and physical energy goes into survival and grieving. Progress is made in such microscopic increments. Then, one day you look up and begin to recognize a new you . . . and it seems impossible that only a few years, not a lifetime, has gone by.

My thoughts today, as I travel toward the four year mark, are on the resilience of the human spirit and how indomitable we truly are. During the course of the past 42 months we have been witness to Oklahoma City, countless murders (including the much publicized deaths of Ron Goldman and Nicole Brown Simpson), the crash of TWA 800, and now the death of Ennis Cosby. Plus, how many quiet, unpublicized deaths have occurred leaving how many broken, grieving parents and siblings in their wake? Our numbers grow daily and, as we move further into this indescribable place, we are brought back again and again to the beginning . . . to the very dark, unspeakable beginning of a journey of our own metamorphosis.

Peter was our only child. He and I had a particularly unique and close relationship. He was, more than anything, my best friend and, I thought, my reason for living. I was recently reminded of how I used to answer people who asked how many children I had. "One!" I declared proudly. "I did it right the first time!" How innocent. How arrogant I was then. How unaware of the possibilities. Now the question strikes me as an intrusion and brings on an immediate hostility. It's really none of your business I want to say, but I don't. "I had one," is my standard answer now. It usually stops people in their tracks. They don't dare go further.

When I think that it is only 3½ years since Peter's death, I am astounded at the progress I've made towards hope. Whereas in the beginning I thought my survival would be a betrayal of my love for Peter, I've begun to understand what so many Compassionate Friends have described. I still do have a son. He just happens to live inside me. In my mind he is very much alive and everything I do is still being judged by him. But make no mistake, it will never be enough. I'll miss his wedding and my grandchildren. I'll miss him helping me through my old age. I will always miss talking to him on the phone and laughing with him, and cooking for him and looking at him. Always—with awe and wonder at his accomplishments. I'm so sad and angry that he is missing a life.

But I live on. I never stop wondering how, but I have become at ease with my despair and more comfortable with hope . . . hope that the day will go peacefully, hope that I will get some measure of pleasure or satisfaction from the people I meet, the work that I do, the movies that I see, the books that I read, the places that I go, the plans that I make.

As you can see, these thoughts could never be understood by the uninitiated. But to those of us who have entered into this uncharted place, to find others that have entered here only just before us, who reach out to help us find our footing, even while they continue to grope towards some inexplicable peace for themselves, gives us hope. Hope that the pain will become more manageable. Hope that we can find a measure of peace, hope that with dignity and grace we can continue our lives as tribute to our lost children.

LOOKING UP

> *I looked up from my sorrow,*
> *Wiped tears aside and found*

FIRST YOU DIE

The day was new, the sun shone on
The world would still go round.

"How can this be?" I screamed and cried,
I'm sure to fly apart!
The center of my world is gone,
A stave goes through my heart!

I've got to learn survival, I reasoned
Through the pain.
My loved ones need me to go on
To share their lives again.

To laugh once more and plan ahead
For living, future times.
I had to think of some way I
Could WANT to start that climb.

And too, among the things HE loved
In me lest I forget,
My humor, spark, my drive and strength
When troubling times beset.

I looked up 'cross that table there
And into eyes that cried,
So pained (like mine), so deep in grief—
Your loved one's too had died.

And in the midst of so much hurt,
My heart felt such concern
For each and every heartache there,
We've all so much to learn.

And as I listened, shared and wept
Together with you all,
A tiny light was lighted and
Some weight began to fall.

None of us is healed or whole,
We've not emerged brand new.
But we're surely somewhat stronger now
In what we seek to do.

My friends, I've gathered strength from fears
I saw there in your eyes.
In quiet ways we've learned to help
Each other realize.

That looking up through veils of tears
We still can vaguely see
And help some other friend "look up"
THANK YOU for helping me.

Kay Daphne Redcoff

LIGHTING THE WORLD
Rambling Thoughts On Fearsome Times
Fall 1999

When the light of a young life goes out, the world gets
a little darker. As we move along in our lives, and the
burdens of time dim the outlines of our idealism, we look to
our children, indeed, the world's children, to brighten our
days and sharpen our vision of the future. When our own

children died we all saw our world darken almost beyond imagining.

This summer we saw three very bright lights go out: JFK Jr., Carolyn Bessette Kennedy and Lauren Bessette. And we, survivors all, were intimately, totally involved in the event. We knew. Unwitting participants, we knew the pain that will never end for the families who went from the light to the total blackness of incredible, indelible, eternal dismay and darkness. We, who have looked back at the light from a distance those who have not traveled here can imagine, knew all about the pain. We didn't need the cameras and the commentators to explain anything to us.

When John Kennedy Jr. flew his plane and its precious cargo of future promise straight into the sea, it was astounding on so many levels that one is hard pressed, even now, to take a breath and try to understand the enormity of what everyone felt. I, for one, was amazed at the intensity of my own pain. After all, having lost our only child, a son who was to us, every bit as handsome, smart and promising as JFK Jr., I didn't believe it was possible to ever be as intensely moved by death again. But life, as we all now know, is full of surprises. I was devastated to my very core. Flashing back to my own tragedy, I spent tearful days and those familiar, semi-sleepless nights that we all know so well . . . waking every 10 or 20 minutes to discover that yes . . . it was true . . . he was still dead . . . and crying myself back to sleep for the millionth time.

The shocking news on that tragic July morning came three days after we had marked what would have been

Peter's 28th birthday. We had been to the cemetery the day before and were reflecting on the cruelty of fate, when we put on the TV to hear the dumbfounding news that the little plane was missing. On board were not only JFK, Jr. but two beautiful sisters. While the world focused on the horrific possibilities, visions of the mother of these two girls kept rising to the forefront of my mind. I could really feel her agony. As I could feel Caroline Kennedy's agony. My bereaved sibling friends have made me acutely aware of that pain and confusion as well.

The hours turned into days. Then, after a week of mind numbing tragedy, I became acutely aware of all the "grief experts." And then, the desperate attempt on the part of all the commentators to find someone who could neatly explain the pain and the resulting sensibilities on all the participants . . . the parents, the siblings, the relatives, the friends . . . the casual observers. We want so desperately to package the pain. To be able to take it out and look at it. To turn it this way and that and understand it. Then put it away in some mental attic until another disaster strikes and we are reminded, once again, that we know all about it.

It seems strange, but the world of grieving has changed considerably since my grandmother lost her own little 2-year-old daughter at the beginning of this century. Through family lore I learned of how this calamity caused her to have a "nervous breakdown" before she could "get on" with her life. A life that included the care and feeding of her two surviving young sons. My mother's birth followed, and then a fairly prosaic life raising her three children. More than 50 years later, when I was a young teenager, my

Uncle Sam died suddenly at the age of 59 and the family decided to have the funeral before telling my grandmother. They were afraid that the reality of losing another child might have killed her. (Yeah? So?) So unmentionable was death, and so misunderstood the need to process the event by acknowledging it, my family thought it would be better left unsaid. For most of this century, the focus was on how to proceed with life without much attention to death. My then 80-year-old grandmother survived for another six years but never really forgave her family for excluding her.

And it was this way until recently. TCF was formed accidentally, a result of two grieving families discovering that it was helpful to commiserate with the similarly afflicted. I am grateful to be surviving in a post-TCF world. But since our son died in 1993, it seems as if there has been such a marked escalation in the death of children. Whole industries have risen around what has become an all too possible tragedy. Toxic waste dumps that cause illness and death, cars, drugs, sex, guns and rage . . . and we keep asking how can we go on? Now, we have cadres of professional grief analysts who have managed to neatly categorize the many "stages" of grief. Because we, the surviving parents and siblings, are so legion and so "out there," grief and the grieving are now recognized and acknowledged as a unified target group for commercial grief counselors. Soon, it would seem, so many of us will have had a close encounter with the unmentionable loss of a child, never again will the phrase, "You'll get over it!" be heard in the land. I suppose that is a good thing. But what does it say about a society that recognizes the remaining families of a dead child as a "constituency" . . . a target audience.

All that being said, I guess what amazes me the most are my own responses to the continuum of "life" as we now know it. What once was impossible is now entirely possible. Nonetheless, even with that knowledge coloring all of my days, how shocked and dismayed I can still be at yet another monumental loss. Children continue to light the lives of parents and families everywhere. I don't resent it any more. I am glad and afraid all the time. And once in a while a young life glows so brightly it seems to make the whole world a bit lighter. Even for us. And then, again, in an instant . . . sudden darkness. What fearsome times we live in.

STAYING ALIVE & REINVESTING IN LIFE

By the end of 1994, 17 months after Peter's death, I began to accept the fact that I wasn't about to die. Half way through my second year of grieving I had figured out some of the things I was going to have to do to re-design my life.

Keeping busy was a priority. The time I spent working convinced me that a steady job would be the best therapy. But I still didn't have the ambition or the wherewithal to seek significant employment. What I thought I needed was a simple job that would force me to get up, get dressed and get out of the house. Activity that would take precedence over brooding became a goal.

Early in 1995, my opportunity came when an old business friend called to ask if I was ready to go back to work. A friend of his needed help right away. It sounded like the simple job I was seeking—personal assistant to the president of a women's clothing manufacturer. I took the job and found myself in the midst of a close knit family company, with many young women whose desks were adorned with the photos and artwork of their offspring. Whenever conversations erupted about the trials and tribulations of parenting, I would beat a hasty retreat. No need for anyone to know about my personal life, I thought.

Before long as I got more involved in the business and my co-workers, who still knew nothing about me, began to ask "where did I come from?" I had asked my employer not to tell anyone about my circumstances, believing that people would judge me or feel sorry for me if they knew I was a bereaved parent.

However, one day I left the office with a co-worker who lived near where I lived. We shared a taxi and, in that intimate space, she finally had me captive long enough to ask if I had children. Recognizing this was a natural curiosity, and feeling a sense of inevitability, I divulged my "secret." My child had been killed in an automobile accident. "Please don't share this information with anyone else," I pleaded, although I knew that would not be the reality. And, as it happened, no one in the office ever asked me again. My co-worker had done me a favor in telling just one of her trusted friends in the office. In no time at all, everyone knew.

It turned out to be good thing. I became comfortable in the knowledge that everyone knew—no longer threatened by that dreaded confrontation. Moreover, I was soon comfortable enough to place Peter's picture on my desk. It was the beginning of a new point in my grieving. Realizing I could again include Peter in the interactions of my daily life brought me a measure of comfort I hadn't anticipated. My co-workers acknowledged Peter's photo, and I felt free to talk about him and share my experiences as a mother of a young child many years before. Peter was now part of a new family of co-workers and friends. Though they never knew Peter, they wanted to know him and encouraged me to share some of the funny experiences we had through the years. Finding myself in the midst of so many compassionate people was extraordinarily fortunate. Their friendship and acceptance went a long way toward putting me on the road to healing. For not only did it allow Peter's existence to come to life, in its way, it brought new life to me as well.

Still, life as a bereaved parent never ceased flaunting its different sensibilities. Simple things like taking a walk, going to some familiar place, or hearing a familiar phrase, could send me down to incredibly low depths from which I would then have to expend enormous energy to recover. Life became a minefield of distractions.

FORBIDDING PLACES
Winter 1998

An odd twist of fate recently put me on a jury with an old friend. Though we have known each other for more than twenty years we had never really had an opportunity to share any serious time together. Now, not only were we on a jury, we were actually sequestered overnight, It gave us some serious talking time and boy did we catch up. Audrey is an incredible gal. It was she who showed up at my home a week after Peter's death with a book, written by her friend Marilyn Heavlin. The book, called Roses In December, opened a door for me that works to this day.

Anyway, during one of our animated conversations that jury week, we began to discuss something that we probably should have avoided mentioning. Audrey immediately admonished me, "Don't go there!" I had never heard the expression before but immediately knew what she meant. We changed the subject.

Since that day I have heard the expression "Don't go there!" many times. I don't know where it originated but it stops us cold when our conversation begins to enter uncomfortable or forbidden terrain. I think of the phrase now, whenever it is suggested that I go physically to certain places. I want to shout, "I don't go there!" Perhaps you too have places you simply cannot go.

I was in California visiting my sister when Peter was killed. She and I had spent the day in Carmel, and I remember having afternoon tea there and talking about the kids (her son and daughter, my niece and nephew, and Peter). We were waxing sentimental about the future and I wondered aloud to her about Peter beginning to discover I could not walk on water. He was my greatest fan. She laughingly assured me that he would always feel that way about me. We couldn't possibly have imagined that, even as we had that conversation, Peter lay dead in New York. We drove back to her house at the end of a perfect day . . . my last.

My memory of what transpired that evening as I learned of the accident is so vivid that the mere suggestion that I visit California brings on a torrent of Technicolor memories that takes my breath away. A friend who recently went to Carmel on business unwittingly caused me considerable discomfort when she related some information about the trip.

Peter was killed on the East River Drive as he was being driven home by a friend. He died at 32nd Street, near The Water Club. I have not driven on that road since and, as much as I loved going to The Water Club in the summer, even looking at it from afar becomes an act of superhuman effort. Quite simply, I don't go there.

I guess it is a luxury to have a choice about where we "go." After all, being in this place that we all now inhabit is most surely a place we would never have willingly gone. I can imagine myself—before all this happened—wanting to say "Don't go there" to anyone broaching the subject of the possibility of bereaved parenthood. But here we are. With no possibility of getting away. So how do we explain to the uninitiated that, once here, there are places one simply cannot get back to.

What we can do is learn how to negotiate this new terrain. We learn survival tactics that often appear selfish and uncaring to the casual observer. We protect ourselves by becoming wary or even by fleeing situations that may add to the already unbearable agony of unstoppable grief. We continue on and elicit the praise of the casual observer who commends us for our courage (what the devil does that mean?), even while they condemn us for our unwillingness to enter places we know will be emotional minefields. Life continues to present daily challenges and we must rise to them. We hear about weddings, bar mitzvahs, graduations, grandchildren . . . we smile. We offer congratulations and gifts. We are happy for them. All from a far off place. A forbidding place. Most people don't go there.

CHOOSING TO LIVE

Two years after Peter's death, my new life was beginning to take on a new shape. My personal grieving process had involved getting in touch with my new self—learning what *I* needed to survive. I had discovered that by writing what I was feeling, I eased the burden of trying to hold on to so many despairing thoughts. I recognized that once I removed these thoughts from my head, by resting them on paper, I no longer feared forgetting, which was one of my greatest worries, one that many bereaved parents share. In writing I could preserve those feelings that I thought I might want to go back to and review at a later time, when I might be able to process my thoughts more coherently.

During this period, I also became an avid gardener and, in so doing, found peace in the renewal of life that I witnessed each season. The physical energy expended in the garden also gave me a sense of nurturing. I began to feel very responsible for the care and feeding of the small piece of the planet that we had acquired just at the beginning of Peter's too short life. When I was in the garden I not only felt Peter's presence, I sensed his approval as well. I needed this approval and the feeling that he was proud of me. All of my efforts . . . writing . . . gardening . . . trying to help my fellow travelers at The Compassionate Friends . . . gave me a renewed sense of purpose.

Being Peter's mother had always seemed like enough for me. With Peter absent, I needed an enormous amount of activity to fill the void that his loss left. I struggled then, and I continue to struggle, to keep occupied with meaningful and satisfying tasks. In doing so, I have chosen to go on living, something that for many years I never thought would happen.

ANNIVERSARIES
Fall 1997

Seems that all of my civilian life, anniversaries were happy milestones. Matter of fact, there were two major celebrations in everyone's life (so I thought) . . . birthdays and anniversaries. Both occasions warranted the same things. A party, a card, a dinner and/or a present. Those were such simple times.

Now I'm in a very different place. Anniversaries are so momentous and so dreaded. They conjure up a collection of mixed emotions. I spend so much energy bracing myself for each joyless anniversary. And then I relive everything. For days before I remember. He was alive, I think. On the day before I relive each hour. On the anniversary date, every painful minute becomes a flashback of details. The day after it continues and, for practically a whole week, I am brought to tears as wave after wave of despair overcomes me. The flood eventually subsides. Floods always do.

I write this having just returned from my Compassionate Friends meeting. I realized, as we went around our circle, that I had been absent for several meetings and that there were many newly bereaved parents attending. I thought back to my first few months and my bewilderment as parent after parent declared the loss of their child . . . one year ago, two years ago, three years ago . . . so much agony . . . so many painful anniversaries.

I remember thinking back then at my own beginning, as I listened to those who had endured three months, one year, two years, five years . . . "How did they do it? They're different from me. They survived to be over it!" What a confused jumble of thoughts and emotions. If only I could fast forward all these newly bereaved parents to where I am today. It's more manageable now. I want to whisk them into the future. And then I think, "Maybe that's what Peter thinks now."

This summer marked four years since I have spoken to my beloved son Peter. It is ever a wonder to me that I go on. For my husband and me, the summer evokes one date after another . . . a regular endurance test of emotion: Peter's birthday is July 14th; Our wedding anniversary August 2nd; Peter's "anniversary" a scant 5 days later . . . August 7th. As you can imagine, we go through a lot of candles in a very short period of time.

But time does indeed tell a lot. Though I marvel that I endure . . . I do. Though my grief hasn't abated as I originally thought it would, I have become expert at managing the pain. This particular summer has brought home an inescapable fact of life. Time flies. Everywhere I go, this summer more than ever, I've listened to people remark on how fast the summer has gone. I wonder. Has it?

Has this summer gone faster than most? Four years ago I thought time stood still. I would sit on the edge of my bed

*for what seemed like a few minutes, transported by despair.
Then I would look up and the afternoon would be almost
gone. Where had the time gone? Now, four years later I
find there is hardly any time at all. My days are filled with
as much activity as I can cram into twenty-four hours. I
realize that no one gets out of here alive, there is so much to
do and so little time . . . and I am comforted to know that.
However far away or ahead of me Peter is, I am rapidly
gaining on him.*

*So I go on. Racing along at 78 RPM. Slowing down only
briefly for a few weeks in the summer when the pain of
another clump of anniversaries clogs my path, chokes my
breathing and time seems to stand painfully still for one
more cosmic moment.*

Spring, a time of the year that invariably brings joy and
happiness to everyone coming off a cold, dreary winter season,
became a most difficult passage for me. Though time has
reinstated my positive anticipation of longer, warmer days
and briefer nights, in the early years of my grieving it was not
always the case.

SPRING AHEAD
Spring 2002

*It is Spring once again. A time of renewal and rebirth. It is
also a time of re-invention. As those difficult Mother's Day
and Father's Day commemorations approach, I am once
again shaking my head . . . this will be my ninth Mother's
Day without my son. Where did the years go? And who
am I now, so different from the woman I was in 1993.*

Several years ago, a newly grieving father sat in our circle and plaintively asked when he would be himself again. As if there was ever a possibility of that. I remember the group telling him that while he felt as if he had shattered into a million pieces, time would eventually enable him to "put himself back together." But, like a vase that's been glued together, he would always bear the scars of the injury. He would never be like his old self again.

We are always under that pressure. Our families, our friends long for us to recover. They pray we will once again be like our old selves. But we know we never will. We can become a fairly recognizable facsimile . . . but there will always be the difference between knowing what we now know and the old innocent souls we were.

People still innocently ask if I have children. I don't hesitate any longer when I tell them my son is dead. They still reel. I don't. They still say, "I don't know how you do it." I still wonder what "it" is that I do. I guess the fact is that I "do" life. What choice do I have? I holed up a long time in my despair. I missed a lot of sunrises and sunsets. Then one day, I felt like Peter was watching me and he wasn't happy. I think I realized then that I was living for two and I made a Herculean effort to re-engage in the world. I'm glad now that I did. Eternity will come soon enough.

The Spring used to mock me. In spite of the hurt and anger I felt, the world seemed to leap at the opportunity to heal and regenerate after a cold dark winter. I felt like an outsider everywhere. Winter hung on my soul like a shroud. It's different today. I realize that I have traveled a very great distance from the disconnected, grieving person I was then. Time has indeed made a very big difference. Now I know Peter is with me every day, accompanying me on an imaginable journey, cheering me on, waiting for me, proud of my little successes. I miss his presence, sharing with him, touching him, hearing him laugh, listening to his plans. I wonder always what he would be doing if he were living his life. Would he be married? Where would his career path have taken him by now? What car would he be driving? Where would he be living?

But I look at the wonderful relationships I've developed in the past eight years as gifts from Peter. Surely it was he who arranged for my friendship with the young couple whose two little children I love and refer to as my adopted grandchildren. Surely it was Peter who arranged for me to become Vika's godmother. And certainly it was Peter who maneuvered a young handsome man into our lives, who has become like an surrogate son to us, complete with the emotional ups and downs of failed romances and the growing pains of early lost love.

While I continue to work, the garden remains my refuge. It is here, alone with the birds and the bugs, that I am most at peace. I talk to Peter and sometimes I can almost hear him responding. I delight in seeing the garden come back to life. It is a constant in a world rocked by insanity. I grieve for all the newly bereaved parents who must now travel this same path. I am so different from the person I was. I'm more forgiving of those whose challenges often cause them to make poor decisions. And I'm more impatient with those who don't see the "big picture" and squander their precious time as though they had a thousand years to live. Judgmental before my world was rocked, I now feel entitled to my impatience. Now I forgive myself first.

It's Spring. The continuum of life abounds. It seems distinctly possible I've been here before. And just as possible, as the perennials that surround me, I'll be back again.

CHAPTER 8: NO SURVIVING CHILDREN

At Compassionate Friends meetings the format often includes breaking into small groups of parents who have suffered the loss of their children through similar circumstances. During my first year there were an inordinate number of parents—probably 20—who had lost their only child. As we told our stories, several parents expressed a wish that there was a surviving child, thinking that might make the experience a little more bearable.

I remember several parents with surviving children exclaiming that having another child made no difference—the pain was as intense. However, that had never been the argument. While other parents would feel compelled to defend their level of grief to be "just as bad" as ours, we knew there were issues we had to deal with beyond the emotional and physical pain of losing our children. While we listened to parents with surviving children exclaim that, "One child doesn't replace another," or, "When you lose an arm it doesn't mean any less because you have another arm." We knew there was a difference.

In our small group we acknowledged that these mindless arguments, designed to measure such incalculable anguish, didn't address the specific issues for those of us with no surviving children. Without having to feel defensive against those who would claim that all grieving parents are alike, our group would share the scarier aspects of our grief.

- We'd never have grandchildren.
- Who would inherit everything we had spent a lifetime building?
- Who would care for us in our old age?
- Who would come visit us in the hospital if we are sick?
- Who would know if we needed help?
- Who would light a candle for us when we are gone?

Knowing there is no one to carry memories of us into the future. We end here. There are no surviving children for whom we can plan holiday celebrations or birthdays. No one to call us "Mom" or "Dad." An integral dimension of our lives is over, ended forever. These are some pretty weighty issues for the grieving—issues that add aspects to grief that make the process even more complicated.

ON LOSING AN ONLY CHILD

During all the years that I've been writing about the state of being a bereaved parent, I've avoided the subject of having become childless in my columns. I remember how overwhelming an issue that was for me during my earliest days. Not only had I lost my beloved child, I had lost everything his life would have brought to mine.

But whenever I brought up my concerns among other bereaved parents, I was often soundly condemned for implying that my grief was greater than theirs. There seemed to be a need on the part of bereaved parents with surviving children to negate the possibility that there was any difference in the magnitude of any bereaved parent's grief.

"Just because you lose an arm or a leg, and have one left, doesn't make it hurt any less," I was told. I had many retorts. Of course the pain is equally intense. But the recovery can be very different when you still have a leg to walk on. Eventually I gave up trying to explain that the loss of an only child, or all one's children, is a singular kind of loss. It just wasn't, and still isn't, "politically correct."

I was fortunate then. (If you can call it that. I use the term loosely.) When I joined TCF, there were five other couples, contemporaries as well, that were suddenly childless. We would form our own small sharing sessions and reflect on the issues we had to face that were unique to our circumstances.

And, though it still isn't politically correct to point out the singularly cruel fate of losing your only child, or all of your children, I have been thinking a lot about it lately. I don't mean to imply that parents with surviving children, or those who can have other children, grieve any less. But I feel compelled here to comment on the issues that so compound the sorrow and pain of this singular loss.

There is no argument that the loss of a child is a grievous loss of such magnitude it cannot be compared to any other. The only greater loss is the loss of more than one child. The pain of each loss is identical. The weight of each loss, no matter the circumstance, is equally immeasurable.

But, just as each loss carries the same weight and heartache, the shape of each loss may differ. Just as we measure a pound of feathers or a pound of lead, we can imagine that it takes a lot more feathers to weigh in at a pound. That pound of feathers comes in a much larger package and may pose a pretty unwieldy burden for the bearer.

So too, the loss of an only child (or children) brings with it a much more complicated grieving process than those with surviving children. (I can hear some readers, even now, ready to chastise me for this suggestion.) In my case, my husband and I lost our 22-year-old son when we were happily ensconced in mid-life and looking forward to our "golden years." Unlike young parents who might possibly have more children (which would not negate the loss, only soften and restore their lives), we knew flat out we were too old. There was no possibility of rebuilding a family.

And so, with Peter's death, we experienced the death of all hope for our future lives . . . no grandchildren; no family celebrations; no more milestones—only anniversaries. Sure there are no guarantees our kids will give us grandchildren, but we all know about hope. How do we come to terms with the loss of all those possibilities . . . all that hope lost? Holidays, birthdays, graduations, weddings, the trials and tribulations, the successes and failures of our kids as they become functioning adults—how do we incorporate the loss of all these future life passages into our remaining lives? It's a daunting prospect.

I think of our, Phil's and my, future milestones—our 50th, 60th, 70th birthdays. Our 30th, 40th, 50th anniversaries. Who will celebrate us? Old age looms big, scary and lonely. Who will be there to advocate for us when we are old or ill or widowed and alone. Not that our children were ever a guarantee of that solace, but with them gone so is the hope that they would be there for us.

And finally, there is the issue of what happens to the sum total of our lives—the bits and pieces handed down through generations or acquired and collected in our own lives. Things collected with the knowledge and comfort and rationale of hoping that much of these material treasures would be lovingly kept by our kids, as reminders of their lives with us. Not to mention the photos. All the Kodak moments from our own childhoods through the lives of our kids. All the days of our lives, all the memories with no future repository. We know only too well, that we too will be gone without a trace.

So you see, the loss of one's children or only child can, and almost always does, present a set of circumstances that complicates the grieving process. Learning to work through the grief and pain, even while dealing with the added burden of the loss of one's futurity, requires an extraordinary effort. Recognizing and acknowledging the existence of these additional emotional burdens on the totally bereaved parent calls for an added degree of compassion that may provide an extra measure of healing for our sadly wounded hearts.

A GODMOTHER?

At my first Compassionate Friends meeting, after going around in a big circle, the participants broke up into small groups, each led by a "facilitator." These facilitators were also bereaved parents who, over the years, had learned something of the territory, and now volunteered to help more recently bereaved parents tell their stories and talk about the issues that were currently affecting them. I had very little to say. It seemed clear to me that I was different from everyone else. In my opinion, back then, no one had a son like Peter, so unique in this world. And I could never sit amongst a bunch of strangers and bare my soul. I decided this venue wasn't for me.

In November of that year, I read an article in *New York Magazine* about the death of a six-year-old boy in Manhattan. It was so touchingly written, and described the story of a child who developed a rare illness and who managed to die a "noble" death by teaching all those who knew him about "love."

It was not a story I would ordinarily have read from beginning to end, but now the death of children had become very interesting to me. I found myself weighing the devastation each death wrought. The death of a baby or very young child seemed to have less weight than the death of an older child. The death of an older adult child could be accepted more because that child had at least "lived a life." It didn't seem possible that the death of a baby could cause the same pain as mine. After all, my loss seemed the most profound.

Only through years of talking to hundreds of grief stricken parents who have lost children of all ages, in ways too numerous to mention, have I learned that the death of a child, whatever age, however many siblings may survive, wreaks the same havoc on a family, and causes the same devastating pain to their surviving parents. It's like the old comparison . . . what weighs more, a pound of feathers or a pound of lead?

Two weeks after the article appeared, the magazine printed a letter from a recently bereaved mother who had also lost her only child, in an accident, a son, 12 years old. Her description of her child so matched mine of Peter, I decided to see if I could locate her. Surprisingly, I easily found her name and address in the phone book, so I dispatched a sympathetic note telling her that I too had recently lost my son and that I really related to her words describing her loss.

Two weeks later she called. We talked and cried on the phone and she asked if I would meet her at the next Compassionate Friends meeting, where she had found some degree of solace. I tried to refuse, telling here that I had been there and found it wasn't for me, but she insisted.

In January 1994, the woman who walked into the Compassionate Friends meeting intent on meeting me looked familiar. This was the same woman who had lost her precious 12-year-old son only seven days before the first meeting I had attended the previous September! We fell into each others arms like long lost friends and have accompanied each other on this difficult journey ever since. Her name is Barbara.

In 1994, one year into our grieving, Barbara began to actively explore the possibility of adopting a child. Her son Shaun—the only child of a single mother—had been killed by a careless driver while the two of them were walking on a country road after an outdoor concert. He had just celebrated his 12th birthday. Barbara had been separated from Shaun's father for several years.

Barbara and I bonded during the earliest days of our grieving. We would attend Compassionate Friends meetings, leave before the meeting ended and repair to a local restaurant where we would share a few drinks with a late dinner and speculate on the absurdity of our lives.

Most absurd to us was that we were still alive. Both of us had a macabre sense of humor. We would contemplate the many clever ways we might end it all. Then we would cry and we would laugh as our plans became more and more outrageous. One night, a diner from another table stopped by our table on his way out of the restaurant to comment on what a good time we seemed to be having! That just made us laugh even harder until tears were rolling down our cheeks. Who would ever believe we had been fantasizing about ending it all?

The truth was that we were both working hard to figure out how to go on. Finally in 1995, sharing a pizza and a bottle of wine, Barbara told me she had decided to adopt the young girl she had gone to meet in Russia a few months before. The girl's name was Vika, and Barbara's big question was would I be her godmother?

I was bowled over. Was it possible that all hope wasn't lost. That perhaps in this life there could be a child I could love and care about and who just might care about me. The moment was charged with meaning for both of us. I was overwhelmed at the possibilities and I knew that my new friend was offering me such a priceless gift. We both recognized that we were becoming speechless. It was too significant a decision, so we both used our greatest strength—humor—to commemorate the request.

"What would it involve?" I asked, stunned.

"Well," Barbara answered with a devilish smile, "You have to attend every major party or event in our lives, and you have to give very expensive presents," she added, laughing.

"I can do that," I declared.

And so the deal was done. Vika arrived in New York a month before her 12th birthday. She didn't speak a word of English and I loved her on sight. The story of her adoption was brilliantly told by her mother in an article she wrote for *Adoptive Families* magazine. Barbara wrote it—*"for bereaved families thinking about adoption, for older children who need homes, in Shaun's memory and for Vika"*

With her permission, I reprint it here.

FROM RUSSIA WITH LOVE
By Barbara Chasen

It was a long, arduous flight from New York to St. Petersburg, Russia. Natasha, an adoption liaison, met a friend and me at the airport and took us directly to the orphanage. The children, dressed to the nines, were being "graduated." Long tables held samovars, tea, and tea sandwiches; the children were putting on a performance. They danced, sang and performed games. It was festive and charming—carpets on the floor, curtains on the window—a far cry from the barren orphanages I had seen the previous year in Romania. Vika, 11, the child I had come to see, was the tallest and the oldest.

Later, when the teachers danced with the children, I asked Natasha if I could join them. She nodded yes. In my jeans and sneakers, clothing worn on the plane, I sidled my way to Vika, who did not suspect that I was there to observe her. As I twirled her, I instantly knew she was a good dancer. Her hair was frizzy. I did not like it. I did not see how really beautiful she was. My friend did.

Overwhelmed with graduation, the director of the orphanage was brusque, demanding an immediate decision about whether I would adopt Vika. Having been in Russia no more than two hours, I told Natasha that I needed to spend more time with Vika to be able to make that decision. I wanted to find out as much as I could about her, which was difficult as she spoke no English; and since she had never attended school, there were no academic records. Natasha was able to get Vika released to go to dinner. Instead, eating a quick sandwich along the way, we went directly to my hotel, where we unpacked and played with various block games. Vika loved them and did very well, persisting until she succeeded, a good sign. I had brought her many presents and gave her a jeans dress with a white shirt, which she changed into immediately. She was sweet, incredibly appreciative, and seemed bright. So far, so good.

The following day, we went to a park. With Natasha translating, Vika and I talked and drew pictures together. Her hair, lo and behold, was not frizzy, but straight and beautiful. She had braided it the night prior to graduation so that it would appear curly. I asked her to write some numbers. For "33" she wrote "30" and "3." My heart sank. Though intelligent, she was uneducated and clearly grossly delayed academically. Could she possibly catch up? That night, my friend, who is not interested in being a parent, jokingly told me she herself would adopt Vika if I did not. I decided to take the plunge.

When I informed the orphanage director of my decision to adopt, her brusque manner shifted dramatically. Out came the samovar, the tea and cookies, and we celebrated. I was numb. A daughter?

But I am ahead of myself.

Never am I far from tears. On September 6, 1993, my dearest 12-year-old son, Shaun, my only child, was killed suddenly, hit by a car. The joy I had in mothering a handsome, brilliant, talented, exceptional child was immeasurable. After his death, I wanted nothing but to die, yet one does not die because one's child does.

I coped with my grief in many ways, fundraising for scholarships, establishing a playground in Shaun's memory. Yet the chasm felt bottomless. Remaining childless, for me, was unthinkable. Too old to conceive again, adoption became my option.

Sometime after Shaun's death, friends began encouraging me to adopt, but one in particular told me of a single mother she knew, a physician, who had adopted a two-year-old from Russia. Quite coincidentally, the adoption agency was located on the west coast in the very small town I happened to be visiting one particular weekend. I made an appointment.

The interview with the adoption agency director started with my showing her pictures of the son I had lost. It was approximately one year after Shaun's death and I was merely putting one heavy foot in front of the other, crying and going through the motions, and not feeling like a very suitable adoptive mother. The director was empathetic and revealed that she herself had adopted two children, and while one had made a wonderful adjustment, the other had some emotional difficulties. This intimacy made me feel less vulnerable on the one hand, other people had problems too; and more vulnerable on the other hand. I did not want to adopt a child with emotional problems. I agreed to start the preliminary paper application, the next tiny step.

After I returned to New York, the agency sent a seemingly never-ending list of things to do, one of which involved a home study. No one had studied my home prior to my having given birth to my son, and it was irritating to be subjected to such scrutiny now at such a vulnerable time. However, since I had been a "successful" mother, I had no doubt I would pass the interview, until some bereaved parents I knew told me they had "failed" their home study because their social worker felt that they had not sufficiently recovered from their grief. Even 1½ years later (time is measured from before Shaun's accident and after), I had not sufficiently "recovered" from my grief, nor did I ever think I would. I wondered how far into the home study it would be before I started to cry.

It took approximately one minute. That my child was dead, that I needed to pass an interview to get a child, and that I was, in fact, in the process of obtaining another child was unbearably painful. The social worker was exceptional, able to perceive my strengths better than I at the time. She reassured me I had "passed," and that she would recommend my suitability as an adoptive parent.

As I was older, single, and bereaved, I felt it would be

one less burden, for the child and me, if the child would look somewhat like me, and not be obviously adopted. While filled with admiration for those who adopt transracial or special needs children, I was simply unable to cope with those variables. It is, however, very difficult to adopt Caucasian children in the United States. Therefore, I chose an international adoption, in Eastern Europe. The paperwork involved—income checks, character references, finger printing, child abuse clearance— kept me busy. A trifle less time for grief.

After two disappointing trips to Romania in February 1995, and to Russia some months later, the agency informed me of the availability Vika, an 11-year-old girl in St. Petersburg, Russia. Pessimism reigned. Perhaps I just ached to have Shaun back, and this all was an expensive exercise in futility. Yet, guardedly, as summer approached, I decided to go to Russia. A friend of Russian Orthodox origin agreed to come with me. She would sightsee, having no interest in children, and I would visit orphanages, having no interest in sightseeing.

A DAUGHTER???

The next morning, on the way to discuss adopting Vika, Natasha told me the Russians had just instituted a new law that compelled all adoptive children to be listed on a central registry for a mandatory period, enabling Russian families wanting to adopt to have first choice of Russian children. Aware of the imminence of this law, I had been reassured St. Petersburg was exempt and still operating independently from Moscow. Now, just as I was about to commit, I was being informed that my adoption was not exempt. With visions of infamous Russian bureaucracy, I saw six months turning into a year or two. Vika, already 11, could be as old as 13 when the adoption finalized, and I feared that would really be too old. I was hoping for a few years of relative calm together before teenage turmoil. I decided not to discuss the adoption with Vika. The rest of the week was spent getting to know each other better, some sightseeing, more presents, a promise to write.

Secretly I was afraid I would change my mind when I returned home. But I did not. I could imagine her in Shaun's room. I could imagine calling her my daughter. Not one to sit idly by, I made many attempts to circumvent the six-month waiting period, writing letters, making telephone calls, all to no avail.

Meanwhile, I sent Vika three to four letters a week, enclosing stickers and silly little presents. The superintendent of my building, Boris, happily, was Russian, and he translated. One day a friend suggested I talk to Vika on a cassette tape. I protested she did not have a tape recorder. He persisted. "Send her one!" I did. Me, one sentence; Boris, one sentence. It was one of the better things I did. Vika still did not officially know I wanted to adopt her, but she was ever alert; and Natasha told me she knew something was up.

Then, one day, when it appeared the wait would, in fact, be not longer than six months, I faxed a letter through Natasha telling Vika that I wanted to be her mother. I asked Natasha to translate and audiotape Vika's response. This time I did not ask Boris; I wanted Vika to hear words from my heart in a female voice. Several weeks later I received an audiotape response. "Da, da, da, yes, yes, yes." Hearing Vika say that she wanted me to be her Mommy, and that she would "never, never, change her mind," gave me the strength to continue waiting.

I repainted the apartment. That was very hard. It was paint that Shaun knew. I cleaned his closet. That was much harder. I sorted things that would be given away forever, or given to Vika. I rearranged the photographs in the room. Unable to take pictures of Shaun down, I put them on one side of the room and her pictures and drawings on the other side, hoping I was making the right decision. One snowy day I bought her a totally extravagant, fancy black flowered chiffon dress at Bloomingdale's and hung it in the closet, envisioning her in it. Faxes flew back and forth. More forms needed to be notarized, certified and apostilled. Who ever heard of apostilled? My birthday was March 20th, and I was hoping to celebrate in Russia. Finally, Natasha said to come.

The trip was, of course, delayed three times due to bureaucratic snags, but at last, once again, eight months after meeting Vika, I boarded the plane to Russia. This time, I went alone. During the months of anticipation, I kept busy buying toys, socks, gloves, t-shirts, candy and stickers. So did some friends. Gifts for her classmates, as well as clothing for Vika. She would be given to me with nothing. I would be staying with Natasha, by now my comrade in struggle and good friend. 17 years prior, she too, had lost a child, a three-year-old daughter, from appendicitis. Subsequently she had a son, Andre, now age 17. Natasha and I had cried about our dead children and had bonded in a very special way.

The next morning, Natasha and I went to various high level administrators to sign official adoption papers. In the late afternoon, we finally headed to the orphanage to pick up

Vika. We spotted each other and hugged and hugged. I gave Vika new clothes, everything from underwear and tights to a hot pink turtleneck, hiking boots, and a new winter jacket. In the excitement, I had forgotten her new jeans. She was, fortunately, able to wear an old pair. We then went to her classroom where the children stood up when we entered the room. They knew she was leaving and were silent, in awe. Vika proudly distributed presents to each of her classmates. Then they chattered happily about their gifts. More hugs and promises to write and we were off.

We drove directly to the fanciest place I could think of, the Café Europa, for tea and the most delicious pastries, and to expunge the feel of the orphanage. Just a few more bureaucratic hurdles left, but already I felt as if Vika were mine. I gave her a Princess Barbie doll; me, a feminist. She loved it.

I wanted Vika to remember her last days in St. Petersburg as happy ones, so the next two days were spent shopping, sightseeing and buying presents for everyone back home. Our first moments alone, after Natasha left, were on the overnight train to Moscow. On our own with no translators, we ate chocolate, the universal language. It was awesome having the total responsibility for this trusting little girl. With the train jiggling, there was no sleep the entire night.

In Moscow we were met by a new host family and taken to their apartment. The last morning we saw Lenin's tomb and got caught in a maze of Russian construction and bureaucracy. Vika, unreassurable that we would not miss the plane, tugged at me angrily and impatiently as if she were the adult needing to take care of me. Terrified as she was to get on the plane, she was more terrified that we would not make it. We did. The flight was a delightful one, filled with newly adoptive parents and their children, the six-month moratorium having just been lifted. Vika held tight to the arms of the chair as we took off. She made friends instantly with a teenage Russian girl, adjusted her headphones to rock 'n roll music, and with her American clothes on, looked as if she had flown every day.

We arrived in New York, going through immigration because of Vika's Russian passport. Then we were home. My mother and two close friends met us with balloons and stuffed animals, Russian tapes for the car and hugs and kisses. At the apartment there were bows and "Welcome Home" signs on the door. Much excitement coupled with fatigue and numbness. Where was Shaun?

I was easily able to hire a Russian/English speaking babysitter who was waiting for us at home to help with translating. Hungry and tired, I ordered pizza. Vika took one look at it and decided to go to bed. In her bed. In Shaun's bed. Would I ever be able to call it Vika's room? I got up in the middle of the night, still on Russian time, and found my mother reading a story to her new granddaughter.

Everything that first year felt schizophrenic. Every first for Vika was also another event without Shaun. I thought adopting a daughter would make it easier, and it has, but she is like him in many ways. I put her in ballet class, but she likes karate, his love. She is artistic. So was he. But she talks more than he did, and she is a fabulous dancer. He was shy about dancing. Jarring, poignant similarities and differences.

Recently I went to a holiday dinner with my bereavement group. The group generously asked to see pictures. When you are grieving for your own child it is very painful to look at pictures of someone else's child. I had not brought any. But Vika's godmother, a fellow bereaved parent, did have pictures and proudly showed them. Pain at a celebration; celebration at pain.

This has been a time of many firsts; Vika's first Thanksgiving, a big family dinner replete with turkey; my first Thanksgiving with a daughter; her first Halloween with a party for her classmates. We snuggle and watch TV together. We are really mother and daughter, yet I know the fullness and richness of a shared history is just beginning.

Vika knows full well about Shaun. Pictures of him are in her room. She has seen me cry and has comforted me, though I do not want to burden her with my grief and try to be careful. I try to comfort her in her losses but, for herself, she currently prefers to forget her past. I do not want to forget mine. The other night she showed me a Chanukah candle for school on which she had written: "This is in memory of my brother who died." I was deeply moved.

It will get better, easier, different. It already has. I'm not sure I look forward to it. In some crazy way, the pain keeps Shaun with me a little while longer. But, the dreadful silence that Shaun's death brought is gone. There's laughter, food, cooking, babysitters, friends, telephone calls, parties, all the accoutrements of a normal life. People have told me what a lucky girl Vika is, but I know that she has given my life meaning again.

Now, instead of a son, I have a daughter. Life can turn on a dime.

ALTERED STATES
Winter 2001

From the time we are born, our personalities are shaped by our chemistry, our environment and our experiences. Our state of mind is a result of these human factors. My life, until Peter's death in 1993, had a typical series of "ups" and "downs." My perspective and my responses were molded by my chemistry, my environment and my accumulated experiences. But nothing in my life prepared me for what was, is—and always will be—a calamitous experience so devastating that it has chemically rearranged me into what might be termed an altered state.

In the beginning, my confusion was so total I had no desire to go on living. Peter, an only child, was the core around which my life and my future revolved. With my future removed I was incapable of redesigning my life. With Peter gone, I found myself in unexplored territory with no desire to learn to navigate or survive. With no surviving children to motivate me, it took my grieving husband (now fearful of losing me too) to remind me that as long as I lived, Peter would live. That thought, giving Peter's memory life, is what gives my altered life meaning to this day.

No one who has not lost a child can imagine how we, the terminally bereaved, look at life. Ours is a perspective permanently changed by catastrophic events impossible to have anticipated . . . and therefore impossible for us to have even suspected the behavioral changes that might become necessary to survive. It puts us in a place that will remain strange, unfamiliar and unbelievable for the rest of our lives.

Those with no surviving children are particularly impacted, especially at the prospect of impending old age. I remember how my mother was concerned about the material treasures she had lovingly collected throughout her life, as well as those she had inherited from her mother. It comforted her to know that the memories inherent in these artifacts would continue on in the compendium of life, continuing to decorate the lives of her children and grandchildren. For me there is no such comfort. My treasures and the memories contained within them are destined to be scattered in a meaningless dispersal.

In my altered state, I watch the grandmas and the grandpas I see on a winter weekend in Florida, delighting in a visit from their children and grandchildren—a joy and a continuum I will never know. Sure, not everyone has kids. Childless by choice or circumstance, their lives are designed accordingly. Their expectations don't include grandchildren. How do we incorporate that acceptance into lives that always anticipated the futurity of grandchildren?

Old age. I watched my parents deal with it. I dealt with it. With love and concern I accompanied both my parents through the last years of their lives. I did everything I could to make that period in their lives as comfortable and filled with joy as I could. Who will do that for us?

As a meaningful birthday, holiday or anniversary approaches, I listen as my contemporaries talk about the celebrations planned for them by or with their children. Though Peter often referred to these, then future, celebrations, he is gone and we must endure the significance these times might have had—permanently focused on what might have been.

Though years have gone by, and family and friends no longer regard our changed chemistry but simply continue on in their lives, comforted by the fact that we no longer appear bereft, or even sound aggrieved—they continue to share their enthusiasm for all the ongoing joys of their lives, imagining that we are no longer affected—that we have become accustomed to this new re-ordered life. (And, I wonder . . . do I want it any other way? Do I want to be left out of their joy?)

I, for one, will never be accustomed to this life. I don't believe, as senior citizenship looms on my horizon, that I should have to re-invent myself to accommodate the ways of those who continue along in a universe parallel to the one I now inhabit. In my altered state I am changed in how I view the world. Shouldn't those who knew the old, unaltered me, regard me with a added degree of compassion and understanding. Just a touch of reserve in their approach to sharing the added joys their unsullied lives have afforded them? A tiny bit of editing in the way they shout from the rooftops when it is aimed in our direction?

Yes, I am changed in how I view the world. Knowing as I do now, that what was always impossible is indeed possible, I feel as if I am looking back from a great distance of knowledge. Looking back at a world where everyone continues to live lives unscathed by the vagaries of fate. My emotional nerve endings remain barely below the surface and my resilience is non-existent.

At this moment, sitting on the beach, looking out at the ocean, I can feel how removed I am from all those who do not recognize the altered state I am in. It pains me to know that some of those closest to me believe the years have distanced me from the event. But we, those living in this altered state, know that time doesn't impact this new chemistry, this throbbing pain—only our skill at managing it.

CHAPTER 9: IT TAKES A LIFETIME

WHERE ARE YOU?

*Where are you? I have been searching
for your continuation in a space that
seems finished. I have wanted to believe
you still exist somewhere else, somewhere
separate, but near to me.
I need only to look inside. I will find you
there, bright and whole, shining steady at
the end of a silver thread of love that will
connect us forever to the most powerful
truth that has ever been or will ever be.*

Molly Fumia, <u>Safe Passage</u>

A few years ago, another newly bereaved mother joined our group at The Compassionate Friends. She was grieving the loss of her son, Perry, who had lost his long battle with cystic fibrosis. As we all are when we first experience the death of our child, she was "shell-shocked," and perhaps more so because Perry had survived well into his 20's, when all the odds were that he wouldn't live through his teenage years. At the time Perry died, Marion had come to believe that he was going to live a normal full lifetime.

At one of our meetings, Marion told a story that has stayed

with me. One day, a friend of hers for more than twenty years came to visit and offer her condolences. They went for a walk during which time Marion railed at the unfairness of it all. Her friend listened calmly as they walked and, when they finally came to a resting place, her friend put her hand on Marion's shoulder and commiserated with her, ultimately agreeing with her sense of unfairness. Then, quite unexpectedly, her friend was assuring her she would get over it. Marion tells of her horror at her friends statement and of looking at her in disbelief while her friend, with a knowing smile just looked at her and continued . . . "It will just take a lifetime."

It seems that her friend, too, had lost a young child, and though more than 20 years had passed, she too was still grieving the loss. Now, consoling her newly bereaved friend, she was faced once again with the prospect of witnessing another grieving mother try to sort out the pain and the possibilities. After so many years, she had come to understand that only when our own lives end will we cease in our efforts to come to terms with the loss of our children. Until then, we must live out the remainder of our time here as best we can, making the most out of what destiny has decreed to be our fate.

Though Peter is not a "living" presence in our lives anymore, he is still "ever" present. Not a day goes by that he is not referred to in some way. Though all parents enjoy talking about their children, as bereaved parents we have only a limited edition of stories to tell. Despite those limitations, Phil and I have managed to totally incorporate his existence into our lives, often in ways I could never have foreseen.

BITTERSWEET
Winter 2000

And now into the breach. It's the 21ˢᵗ century. We are at the beginning of a new century that will, more than any other in history, see changes in the way life progresses, cultures are managed, economies are grown. We, the terminally bereaved, have crossed over into another world—and we have survived. We have made the jump in spite of our grief, our trepidation, our fears and our incredible sadness.

Oh, what would this brave new world have been like if we could have seen it through the eyes of our missing children, brothers, sisters?

Instead, we are assured of the continuum of grieving. That time does not heal as much as it teaches. It teaches endurance. It teaches compassion. It teaches us survival skills we never imagined we could learn. It teaches us an appreciation of all we had and all it is possible to lose. It teaches us that it is possible to appear to be alive even when so much is dead inside. I can only speak for myself here, for I have no surviving children. My loss was not only of my precious son, it was so much of my loss of self . . . my loss of motherhood, grandparenthood . . . the loss of all I have built in a lifetime that I always believed would matter to some future generations.

In the end, I am left at the beginning of this century, too aware of the end of myself. While my peers and distant relatives are happily marrying off their youngest children

*and enjoying their first grandchildren, Phil and I
contemplate long-term care and anonymous philanthropy.*

*The past seven holiday seasons magnified my loss and
taught me to think of all my compassionate friends . . . those
I know personally, and those I only know through the most
catastrophic news events. This past season, the Millennium
celebrations across each time zone, displayed a world where
it seemed that everyone is young, happy, innocent and
unafraid. For one brief 24-hour period, the planet seemed
to have whirled out of orbit into some wonderful place where
nothing bad happens. No computers glitched. No terrorist
surfaced. But grief is like an internal terrorist. We never
know exactly when it will strike us down into depths of
despair, but we know only too well that it will. Though I
watched all the activity with a smile on my face, I couldn't
shake the interminable sadness that rests right under my
skin, waiting to get me once again.*

*And yet, there are all those fresh young faces, bravely looking
at a future so new, so unknown, so unsullied by personal
history. Deep down I am so excited for them. I want to
draw them all close to me, to try to see a future through
their eyes. For time has taught me that it does go on. As we
approached the turn of the century, I felt an overwhelming
sense once again, of loss . . . that I was leaving my life
behind. That I was unwillingly being carried along by the
crowd, unable to stay in a world I knew.*

*But something strange happened. As the countdown to
2000 grew to a fever pitch, I had a sudden sense that
Peter had leaped across what had become, in my mind,*

an enormous, insurmountable chasm of time. That he was
watching me from a distant future . . . smiling and waving
me on. So now, I march ahead, toward my waiting son,
more determined than ever to live what is left of this life
for both of us.

BEING ABLE TO GIVE AGAIN

Many years ago I worked with a young woman at a design company in the fashion industry. It was her first job out of college. Though she was very young, she was, in my opinion, exceptionally bright, very creative and entrepreneurial. She had a wonderful, positive attitude about everything, and a willingness to learn and a determination to succeed that I instantly admired. It wasn't long before I began referring to her as "the daughter I never had." Her name is Nancy.

During the years we worked together, we formed a comfortable and close association, and I marveled at her perception and talent for someone so young and inexperienced. Eventually she wound up running the company. Shortly after I left and the owner lost control of his business, Nancy and her young husband, Neil, went on to form a company of their own, using the principles she had learned and improving on all the methods.

I had lost touch with Nancy for a few years before Peter died. On August 8, 1993, the day after Peter was killed, Nancy and Neil's first child, Jessica, was born. I received the birth announcement a month later and, though I cared deeply, I was incapable of responding. I finally managed to send a note, explaining my situation and asking that they understand my inability to respond properly, requesting that they refrain from attempting to contact me. I needed time.

Eighteen months later I had managed to pull myself together enough to go back to work when I received an announcement of the birth of Jessica's brother, Willy. Recognizing that I had never properly acknowledged Jessica's birth, I bought gifts for both babies and had them hand delivered to Nancy's office. It took 20 minutes for her to call me and, crying together on the phone, we reestablished a friendship that has brought much of the joy I had been missing back into my life.

TELLING TIME
Winter 1998

We've just turned the clocks back. But only one hour. I think, if only I could really turn the clock back. Like Superman, when Lois Lane gets killed. I think that now, more than any other time in my life, I am constantly reminded of time. How much I've lost, how little I seem to have left.

It's holiday time. As I write, Halloween is days away. By the time you are reading this Thanksgiving will be days away. And then, the roller coaster ride to Christmas/ Chanukah and the final New Year of this Millennium.

I am still brought short each day with the realization that I am moving on through time but Peter is not. At each new meeting I am brought back face to face with the haunting specter of raw, inconsolable, indescribable grief and disbelief. As each newly bereaved parent finds us, I meet myself again and again. And I am, once again, introduced to the effects of time.

In the beginning time stood still. From the moment I learned of Peter's death, and for months after, it seemed as if time had simply stopped. There were days when, lost in a reverie of disbelief, I would suddenly "come to" to discover hours had passed. When I did finally go out of my house alone, I would be startled to find it had taken me hours to get only a short distance from home. Where did that time go?

At the end of my first year of grieving, I often felt as though people expected me to be pretty far along towards healing. My anger and resentment began then, when I realized that time had nothing to do with grieving. A friend, coming to her son's second anniversary, tells me her employer of more than 20 years is pressuring her to go back on a full time schedule at work. She's told by this 30-year-old, unmarried, childless manager, that, "Two years should be enough. Time to get back on track." Another friend, 16 years into her grieving, is startled almost every day when she realizes that in another year, she'll have missed her daughter longer than she had her alive.

A dear, dear friend of mine, a gal I worked with many years ago and who I used to refer to as "the daughter I never had," had a little girl five years ago. She was born the day after Peter was killed. Today, at age 5½, she represents all of time to me. She is the measure of all I have lost. As well as what I've gained.

But it is the chronic, constant reminder of time itself that comes with this territory. Every month brings another marker . . . a birthday, anniversary, holiday . . . the first, the second, the third . . . When do we stop counting? I suppose in the next Millennium.

Meanwhile, we continue to mark the times of our lives. Always with the names, the love and the memories of our beloved children, more remembered than ever.

Over the last ten years I have accepted that, although most of what happens during a lifetime is random and out of our control, there are a few things we can direct. We do have some choices. Though I could not control Peter's life or death, any more than I can control my own, I can take charge of the choices I have available to me on any given day. And, although I wished that my life would end sooner rather than later during those first drowning days after Peter was killed, time has convinced me that the end will come soon enough. That wishing for it is not necessary. After all, no one gets out of here alive. Surviving, making the most of each day, bringing hope and peace into someone else's day, giving life to good memories, making flowers grow, making someone laugh, teaching a young person something about the journey . . . these are all good reasons to go on.

And believing as I do, that someday Peter and I will be together again, making sure he is proud of the way I have chosen to live the remaining days of my life, is my most powerful motivation.

REMEMBRANCE

What is death? Death is nothing at all.
I have only slipped away into the next room. I am I and you are you.
Whatever we were to each other we are still.
Call me by my old familiar name.
Speak to me in the easy way which you always used.
Put no difference in your tone. Wear no forced air of solemnity or
sorrow.
Laugh as we always laughed at the little jokes we enjoyed together.
Play, smile, think of me, pray for me.
Let my name be ever the household word that it always was.
Let it be spoken without effect, without the trace of a shadow on it.
Life means all that it ever meant. It is the same as it ever was.
There is absolutely unbroken continuity.
Why should I be out of mind because I am out of sight?
I am waiting for you, for an interval,
somewhere very near, just around the corner.
All is well.

Rosamund Pilcher. <u>September</u>

BROKEN DREAMS
Spring 2000

Recently someone asked me to write down some of my thoughts about Peter. Who he was, how he was and how he impacted my life. At first thought the project appeared to be a breeze. The question was also asked of Phil. The inquisitor wanted to get a man's view, a father's take, as well as mine. In the almost seven years since he's been gone, I've written and spoken volumes about Peter. To me, writing about him has kept him alive. But now, more than describing him, defining the loss of him may be a more accurate view.

To describe him is easy. He was an adorable child. He was bright, articulate beyond his years, funny and captivating. He grew into a young man of considerable charm, was a caring human being, considerate of his family and sensitive to his friends. Over the years he and I developed a particular rapport. He was so like me, I could anticipate his every response. And my ability to do that always knocked him out. We delighted in each others' company to the point where Phil often felt left out of our little party. I thought Peter was the greatest thing since sliced bread, and he thought I could walk on water. It was a mutual admiration society beyond all explanation.

Peter was still living at home when he died. He had been away at college but, having just graduated, he had not yet gone out on his own. His world was contained within mine. I would still not fall asleep until I knew he was safely home. I was still the one to enjoy all the tales of his day each evening. Though he was a lover and had a significant girlfriend from the time he was 16, my position as the most important person in his life had not yet been compromised. In truth, on the eve of his 21ˢᵗ birthday, he had been jilted by a college sweetheart who, he believed, was going to be "the one." When she left him, it was to me he came and wept. During that last year of his life, he worked hard to get over a broken heart that he exposed to me, his mother, in all its merciless pain and ego smashing cruelty. We became even closer in that year, if that is possible.

And so, to have seen him robbed of his life before he could even heal from the devastation of a lost love so important to him . . . to know he was gone into some unknown never-never land where perhaps, on some level, he might be conscious of my torment . . . this prince, this lover, this marvelous, beautiful, sensitive, caring, tender creature . . . how do I now try to bring my seven-year-old loss into some perspective to those who are fairly convinced that Phil and I are well on our way to (oh, dare I say it?) "closure."

Peter was the most miraculous thing that could ever have happened in my life. I am blessed (or cursed) with an inordinate instinct about life. I always had a sense of life being much bigger, much more than my small place in it. Growing up, they said I had a "maturity" beyond my years. History always intrigued me, especially that of my family. The endless conversations I listened to between my mother and her mother, the family "gossip" and speculation of the goings-on among the family's historical, long gone ancestors were recollections I had always hoped to put into a journal for our heirs. As Peter grew, he became the young

135

participant, listening as my mother and I continued the family tradition . . . carrying tales of the past into a future that Peter now had in hand. It would fall to him to carry these family sagas down to the next generation.

And then, suddenly, in a microsecond, it was all over. Peter killed on a dark, rainy night, the driver of a careening container of death and destruction, blissfully unaware of his possible cosmic impact on the lives of so many innocent victims. As has happened countless times before, and countless times since, Peter, Phil and I were caught in what we all think of as an impossible event. Something that only happens to other people. Something that had never happened to anyone we knew. Something that could never happen to us. Simply said, our world ended.

People say time heals. People say we have much to live for. People say we must get on with our lives. People say we were lucky to have had him for 22 years. People say lots of things. And because of what people see, much of what they say has some truth in it. We look okay, if considerably older (we've each put on about 30 pounds). We seem to be getting on with our lives. We are definitely lucky to have had Peter at all. He was, as it turns out, what life was all about. Now, we simply go on. Some days, we even have a few laughs. And if life, as we now know it, appears to have some good times, those in the know recognize the reality of what is missing. It is joy.

Peter used to regale me with his daily adventures. This handsome person, fully grown, that I clearly remembered as a blob requiring care and feeding, entertained me daily with recollections of his daily experiences of discovery. He shared with me all of his hopes, his dreams . . . all the promise his future held. He kept me young. He chastised me when I came home late. I reveled in his caring for me. And during the stupid years, when young adults realize that only they have all the answers, that parents are a miracle in that they have survived at all without the sage advice of their children, I used to love being told the right way to do things by my treasured child. I loved being his Mom. And I loved being loved by him. No matter what I did, history guaranteed he would still love me. People can say what they will. The loss of that unequivocal love defies description.

And I appreciated him. Without Peter I would never really have understood what my mother and father went through raising my sister and me. It was living through his life that I came to understand my own. And losing him has defined what I have become. I live every day with death as my companion. There is no getting away from it. It colors everything. I see young people, the children of my friends, marrying now. And I watch and wonder what tragedies will befall them in their lives. I hate when that thought jumps into my head. I'm shown photos of the young children of my co-workers and I wonder—will they live into adulthood? Stop! Stop! I tell myself. Someone I know suffers a death in their family. Everyone gets upset. I shrug. I wish I could commiserate more. But I can't. When someone loses a mother or father, I can't be sad. I think of them as having been lucky enough to die without ever burying a child. My perspective on life and what is important has shifted dramatically. And having to conclude how insignificant my life is, with no child or grandchild to remember me or be impacted by my having lived, brings on an almost palpable sadness.

I spend an inordinate amount of time wondering about and planning my own end. I fear for Phil if I die first, and I fear more for me if he dies first. Nothing seems to matter anymore. My passion is gone. I surround myself with pictures of my past. Peter smiles down at me from everywhere. He is ageless. I live in a future I could never have imagined, looking back upon a past that was far too short. There is never anything beyond today. Thinking of the future makes me wistful, often sad. The future is filled with "what might-have-beens." I try to stay in the moment and am daily brought back to what once was. Peter will never call me again. He will not suddenly appear at the door. He will not marry, he will not enjoy even the little that Phil and I have. He won't have a career; he won't make an impression on his children. He will never be a man in full. He will never have my grandchildren. He will not do so much more than he ever did.

Yes, we are getting on with our lives, living while sparing everyone around us what has become our daily reality. But the truth is, life has become quite a balancing act.

CHAPTER 10: RESTORATION

"Time is neutral. What helps is what you
do with time . . . YOU *must help time to do its healing"*

Earl Grollman
Living When a Loved One had Died

L ooking back over the past ten years since Peter died, it seems impossible that so much has happened in the world . . . a world that is no longer Peter's world. So much life and death since 1993.

Peter just missed the great internet explosion, the cell phone, the boom years and the subsequent bust of the high tech industry. The great OJ Simpson debacle, the Oklahoma City bombing, the horrors of Columbine and the murder of Ennis Cosby. He didn't learn of the deaths of JFK Jr. and the Bessette sisters; watch on TV the countless little wars which caused so many big deaths. He never saw the renaissance of Times Square, didn't celebrate the turn of the century, or witness the rise of terrorism and the collapse of the Twin Towers.

It's been an extraordinary decade that I have experienced through the filter of bereaved parenthood. As each untimely death and disaster smashes into my supersensitive consciousness, causing the lightening flashbacks of the desperation and despair that followed me for so long, so too, the little victories and accomplishments carry an inordinate amount of pleasure, no doubt because feeling good is always such a surprise.

Losing a child, along with a myriad of indescribable sensibilities, also causes what may be the most devastating feeling of all, the loss of hope. Unless you have experienced this despair, you cannot fathom the devastation such a loss causes. So it is the slow, steady restoration of hope that marks the road back from desolation.

One might ask "Hope for what?" Why do we need hope at all? Hope is defined as desire with the expectation of achieving what is desired. When Peter died, my desire for anything and everything died too. And so, at first, my only desire was to die so that I could be with my son. It was my only "hope." It was the only way I thought I could eliminate the excruciating pain. In fact, I truly believed I would die and I welcomed the possibility. Being reunited with Peter was the only thought that comforted me. The platitudes being proffered by the friends, family, associates and acquaintances that drifted in and out of my consciousness did nothing to comfort me or restore my capacity to hope. Only time and experience has done that.

AS THE WORLD TURNS
November 2002

Nine and a half years ago, when the world stopped turning for me, I listened, without hearing, to the platitudes offered by those observing my sorry state. When I railed against the heavens, when I begged for release from the pain, when I prayed that I could join my beloved, now dead, child, all anyone could do was stand by and watch. There really was nothing anyone dared say without getting some horrific retort from me. So those who stayed just listened. Most drifted away, unable or unwilling to cope with the despair that emanated from my every pore.

The days were as dark as the nights. Nothing and no one could offer me any hope. And in looking back, it is hope that we all long for. It's taken years and years to heal to this point and, as the painful season of "joy" approaches, I thought I would reflect a little bit, on the journey, the distance and the light that slowly appears at the end of the tunnel. Sure they're all clichés. But as those of us who have lived for years in the world of metaphor know only too well, they are clichés because they describe this place so well.

This will be our tenth Thanksgiving without Peter. That first Thanksgiving I thought it would be a good idea to surround myself with the activity of the day and make dinner for my remaining family. It was a major mistake. The day proved more difficult than I imagined and, for years after, Phil and I refused the company of friends or family and remained sequestered at home with the tiniest turkey we could find. It was several years later, with two other couples, also newly childless, that I attempted Thanksgiving dinner again. And, with my new friends, we all reflected on how grateful we were to have had our kids, even while we continued to rail together at the fates for our mutual misfortune.

The December holidays, hot on the heels of Thanksgiving, brought only more pain. Store windows, newspaper ads, magazines, television, radio . . . the holidays were in my face everywhere I turned. There really wasn't anywhere to hide. It was a painful annual rite of passage. But to where?

No getting around it. In spite of us, the world keeps turning. The holidays come relentlessly every year. Along with all the other special days we must anticipate and endure. But for me, more than nine holiday seasons later, the edge has finally softened. Thanksgiving remains difficult, but not as difficult. We can even enjoy sharing the day with friends. And the beauty of the holiday season, especially in a city like ours, no longer makes me angry. I'm glad, now, to know that so many people are untouched (yet) by tragedy. That they can enjoy the holiday season with the brightness and clarity of innocence. And I suspect now, that so many others are like me. I no longer feel so uniquely tragic.

I am an observer now, not exactly a participant. But from my perspective, high on a perch looking back over so much of life, I can appreciate the wonder, and remember that I, too, was innocent once, untouched by tragedy. And knowing what I now know about life, I look at all the joy and know how tenuous it all is. I've also learned the human spirit is a miraculous thing. And that as the world turns, as night turns into day, despair can turn to hope. As the pain begins to subside, the restorative power of hope returns.

For those who are only recently bereaved, it is important to understand that there is no timetable for healing from our wounds. No formula. For some it is months, some years, some decades. Taking it one hour, then one day, at a time is key. There is no way to rush the process. But finding hope . . . hope that the pain will begin to soften, that despair will lift, that life will once again be worth living, that the thought of our children will bring a smile instead of tears, that just maybe we will be with our children again someday . . . you can be sure the power of hope will return.

The world is still turning. We're just going along for the ride. Rest assured, we all reach the same destination. No need to ask if we're almost there yet. One day, without even realizing, we'll know, because our kids will be there, waiting.

I don't know when it began. I do know it wasn't the first year when almost every day had a singular and empty significance. I also know it wasn't the second year, when everyone who had been so patient and understanding during the first year, began to lose patience with my unrelenting sadness and growing anger. I'm fairly sure it wasn't during the third or fourth or fifth years, when almost every thought and response I had was laden with my sense of being entitled to some deference as a bereaved parent.

Yet, one day, I woke up, my thoughts occupied with some anticipated event of the day and realized, suddenly, that Peter wasn't the very first conscious thought of the day. It had been an hour or two before he invaded my thoughts and perched himself once again at the forefront of my mind. It wasn't much, but it was a beginning.

I noticed that I began to look forward to things. Spring, for instance. Spring, when so much rebirth and renewal surrounds us, offended me in the years following Peter's death. A beautiful day that once mocked me with all its joyful portent, began to sound very appealing. Ultimately, I took refuge in my garden, and the restorative power of watching it come back to life each year became my most successful therapy. Looking forward to a dinner party with friends, avoided for years, became a possibility. Indeed, refilling my address book with newer friends who didn't have the "old me" to compare me to, became another achievement. Traveling away from home on a mini-vacation, once unthinkable, became a reality. And, with each acknowledgement of a positive experience, the seeds of renewed hope were sown.

Yes, life does go on, despite having felt that it wouldn't for so long. I have survived the death of my only child. I will forever grieve his loss of the life he was entitled to. I will forever grieve my loss of the life I was entitled to with him. But time, and great effort, have taught me the lessons I needed to learn about surviving.

It's been a course in pain management and personal reinvention. I am a very different person today than I was. So many of those who knew and loved the old me have been unable to accept the new me and have drifted away. On the other hand, I have met and made so many new friends who truly understand the transformation, for they too are traveling this road. I have found great solace in the friendships I have made at my Compassionate Friends meetings, for these friends require no explanations for anything I say or do. They understand, for they too are in the process of restoring their lives.

GOOD GRIEF
Fall 2001

We have just marked the 8ᵗʰ anniversary of Peter's death. Three weeks ago, we "celebrated" what would have been his 30ᵗʰ birthday with several of our Compassionate Friends. Miraculously, we turned what was an anxiety driven occasion into a beautiful day, celebrating Peter's life and the lives of all our missing children. As I write this I marvel at the distance we've traveled on this remarkable journey. Eight years ago, it would have seemed incomprehensible that a) I would be alive, b) I would be living what appears as a fairly normal, if excessively busy life, and c) that we would have incorporated our beloved, invisible, only child into our remaining days.

The effort of producing the newsletter exposes me to an abundance of writings about grief. One of my greatest sources of information comes from my dear friend Jerry Papkoff, who edits the Brentwood/Santa Monica California newsletter, where his wife Barbara serves as chapter leader. So much of what you read in these pages are discovered in Jerry's newsletter. I recently read an article Jerry found in Bereavement Magazine (Sept/Oct 1999) by Rev. Paul A. Meltzer, called "No Finish Line for Grief." In it, Rev. Meltzer discusses "An appreciation of the fact that grievers form an inner sense of continued bond with deceased loved ones. Survivors hold the deceased in loving memory for long periods, often forever. This inner representation allows a sense of connection and interaction with the physically absent, but emotionally present, loved one. The paradox of grief in their view is that 'good grief' seems to result in both a letting go and a remaining involved."

I think back now to those early days when I feel melancholy and need my grief to be weighted down by tears. I can draw on every vivid detail of the experience . . . learning of Peter's sudden death in a brutal car accident caused by a reckless friend driving on a rain slicked road at a terrifying high speed . . . my keening screams that so damaged my vocal chords I was forced to weep soundlessly for weeks . . . the activities of death . . . funerals, staying home to receive sympathetic callers, praying, trying to comprehend.

I think of the years trying to cope with life without Peter present. Reading all that I could in the hope of discovering this might be a manageable condition, and discovering that I was indeed in the company of millions who were in lockstep with me trying to sort out their own grief. Finding support in attending Compassionate Friends meetings and befriending so many wonderful people willing to share their own experience so that I could learn to manage my own.

I realize now that Phil and I have incorporated Peter so totally in our lives, we barely notice if people flinch when we refer to him, which we do all the time. Because so many of our friends now are also bereaved parents, we all refer to our kids whenever stories are told about past vacations, schools, people we know, people in the news. Usually we laugh. And every little mention keeps our children in the present. Good grief.

I remember, in the beginning, the silence of friends and

family, the unwillingness to speak Peter's name. As if doing so might remind me that he was dead. As if I could forget. And it's the fear of forgetting that is so prominent in our minds. The fear of forgetting what he looked like, or what he sounded like. The fear of forgetting how much it hurt. The fear of accepting the loss. The fear of not grieving anymore for our treasured children.

For eight years now Peter has been my main focus. I wonder what he would be doing. I wonder if he would have been married by now and if I would be a grandma. I always wanted to be a grandma. Instead he is my indelible child, forever 22, unencumbered by the slings and arrows of outrageous fortune. The many memorials we have created in his name, all meant to keep him here, in the present, include an academic scholarship at his high school, an adoption center for the cats he so loved here on earth and a park bench with a brass plaque bearing his name. All good grief.

Through my writing I have introduced him to so many who might never have known him if he hadn't traveled out of this world. Keeping him here in the present time, in a world that should have been his, has become my mission. I'm grateful that I live in a time when it is acceptable to include our missing children in our lives. That we can continue to share memories and stories about them, and not be encouraged to keep the loss to ourselves and "move on with our lives" without them. Phil and I have a ritual. Every Friday night we light a candle that burns for the entire weekend. Our little ceremony includes a mini-conversation with Peter and bids him welcome. We always feel he is with us while the candle burns. Good grief.

There surely is no timetable for grieving. We will always grieve the loss of Peter. But after eight years we've concluded this is probably as good as it will ever get. Peter will never be further away or closer than he is now. Until we meet again.

LIFE GOES ON

I'm living a new life. It isn't the life I had originally designed, but it is the best I can do with what I've been dealt. And it really isn't a bad life. It includes an extraordinary young man who was only able to accompany me for 22 years of my journey. He loved me unconditionally and was the greatest joy I could ever have imagined. I continue alone now, on a path that I am sure will lead me back to him. Along with my hopes for good health for my friends and family, for peace in the world, for my life to have had some purpose, it is the hope that I will someday be reunited with Peter that sustains me.

THE NEED TO MATTER
Winter 1999

On the recent 10ᵗʰ anniversary of the downing of Pan Am flight 103, a surviving sibling wrote a touching tribute to his brother in The New Yorker magazine (December 21,1998), called "Where My Brother Fell to Earth." In the end, after 5000 masterfully written words describing the event, it's aftermath, the effect on the survivors and most poignantly, a lengthy description of his lost brother's failings and attributes, Ken Dornstein ends with the sentence . . . "In the end it can be said that he mattered."

I was so taken with this closing sentence. It pierced my soul with a familiarity that made me feel I could have written it myself. Looking back, I saw that I had. When I could not get the phrase out of my mind, I began to look through much of the pained writings of my earliest grieving days. As memory overcame me, I soon came to recognize my own lifelong desire to matter, and my unrelenting belief that Peter was ultimately what made me matter. And I recognized too, that my hope of Peter mattering in some future extraordinary sense died with him that rainy night in August 1993.

All of us feel, in addition to how much we ourselves matter, that our children make us matter. Without them we are so reduced that, whatever else we ultimately do with our remaining lives, we will never matter as much as we did to our kids. I suspect this need to matter, and coming to terms with not mattering, is more pronounced among those with no surviving children. Surely, the loss itself is no greater when it is one's only child. However, when the loss leaves you childless, that loss becomes a loss of one's self as well, seeming to bring on a sense of being adrift in the universe . . . of simply not really mattering at all.

As a child I can remember thinking how wonderful it must be to be able to write a book. Or paint a painting. Or write a song. Strange as it is to contemplate today, in my earliest years I was impressed by lives that managed to create something lasting beyond their own limited life span. I suspect that the desire to leave something larger than life behind is not limited to the great artists of the day. The poorest kids in the bleakest neighborhoods recognize the thrill of leaving their graffiti "tags" on overpasses, trains and other impossible locations. In their limited view, it is their statement of immortality. Something that will outlast them and give some permanent meaning to their little lives.

By the time I had Peter I no longer believed I would write the great American novel, paint a masterful work of art or compose a body of music to rival Gershwin. But in my child rested all the possibilities of the universe. Not only did he more than fulfill my wildest creative dreams, in him, hidden from anyone's possible knowing, could be some future greatness that could impact the world. It mattered greatly that he survive and prosper for all that might come after him. We all matter for what might come from our having existed.

So how do we, in our almost completed lives, resolve the fact that our greatest work, the one that would have made us really matter, has been lost? That though we may manage to matter temporarily in some tiny way, nothing that will ever happen in the world will be greatly impacted for our having lived. Believing this, it astonishes me, that I, and so many of my bereaved friends, simply refuse to give up the fight. Though Peter is physically gone, I fight daily to keep his memory alive . . . to make him "matter." Though he will never write the great American novel, perhaps one of the kids who benefit from the scholarship award that bears his name will. Those who knew him are regularly reminded of him by me. Those who only know me in my post-Mom life, always tell me that they feel like they know Peter. That is always music to my ears.

The need to matter is so overwhelming to us. To us, our children mattered more than anything in the world. Days after Peter died in 1993, I put together a little book about him, to give to those who loved him and who, I hoped would occasionally give his brief life a thought and glance through the little book in remembrance. The book was modeled on a little book I made for Peter on his 21st birthday a year before. It was filled with photos and affirmations and a letter telling him that he had surpassed all our hopes and dreams for him. Looking back, I'm so glad that I did tell him how astounding we thought he had turned out. In my desperate attempt to quantify so short a life, in the little commemorative version I wrote:

This little book is about a life.
Peter's life.
Though short it was well lived.
He grew up fairly healthy.
He grew to be tall . . . and handsome.
He knew love—the love of his family
And his friends.
He knew of romantic love—
the magic of finding it . . .
the pain of losing it.
He knew passion and physical love.
He knew adventure.
He knew intense brotherly friendship.
He enjoyed great comfort and social acceptance.
He knew the admiration of neighbors and associates
He knew how to be kind and caring.
He knew achievement.
He knew how to laugh and make others laugh.

His was a successful life,
for in the end, it can be said that he mattered.
He had a presence that seemed "larger than life,"
and an impact that will long survive him.
Those who knew him are better for the experience.
Those who come after him will know him
from those who carry him in their hearts.

GOING THE DISTANCE
Summer 2003

I think I get it now. I'm not certain, but I think, that as I approach the ten year mark, I have figured out how to navigate the lay-of-the-land so to speak. What was alien territory and so terrifying almost ten years ago has become familiar and much less frightening.

I remember the early days vividly. It's interesting, that it comforts me to know I can remember the early days. I was afraid back then, that I might forget the pain—and even while I begged and prayed for it to subside—I knew I wanted it, in some strange way to continue. The pain, the despair was a palpable "something" I could almost touch. It was an unbelievable reality I could wrap myself around while I tried to come to grips with the fact I would never have my son to wrap my arms around again. My fear back then, of forgetting the reality of him alive, has been replaced by my acknowledgement of the reality that he is in another place.

Now I am no longer fearful. I know the pain is not only not forgotten, it is never far away.

Another Spring is here. Always a difficult season, I now know what to expect. I know that Mother's Day and Father's Day are embedded (new buzz word) in the season. I don't anticipate those days with great anxiety anymore. I know that no one will celebrate with me. I am no longer "angry" (much) that I am an 'outsider' at that party—no longer entertaining a tiny thought that someone might remember and send me a card. I'm not disappointed anymore because I've become familiar with that reality too. Though I will always be Peter's Mom, Hallmark hasn't tapped into the telepathic market yet.

I've stopped trying to teach the world what it's like. I thought, early on in my journey, that I could somehow show the uninitiated a little glimpse of the territory by writing what I was feeling. But I recognize now that the uninitiated aren't supposed to know. The fates are saving them for themselves. When you arrive in this place you must be a "virgin" griever. No amount of warnings or fears can prepare you for this journey.

It's been almost ten years. Impossible, but still true. When you quantify it, in addition to the more than 3650 days, it includes those heavy duty survival days—ten birthdays, ten anniversary days, ten Thanksgivings, ten Mother's Days, ten Father's Days, ten Springs, ten Summers, ten Christmases and 560 candles—just for Peter.

In all this time, in my quest for understanding, I've come to know hundreds and hundreds of newly bereaved and not so newly bereaved parents. For me, that's been the most helpful learning experience of all. I've learned that we all start off the same way. We arrive here dazed, confused and disbelieving. We all think we may or even want to die. But we really only want to be with our kids again. Those of us who are fortunate enough to find a support system like TCF ultimately discover we are in a graduate survival program for the grieving. But it's years and years before we recognize that.

Time and my own desperate struggle to survive have paid off. Peter is more totally a part of me now than he might ever have been without my hard won understanding of the territory. He is an ever-present fixture in my consciousness, attached to every thought, every perception, every emotion, every feeling, every sensibility. He is my constant companion—motivating me, encouraging me, comforting me—waiting for me.

I'm glad I stayed the course and didn't drop out. I'm ready for my degree. I've learned from those who were here before me, and especially from those who came after me, what it takes to survive. You've all taught me well and I'm still learning. I'm so grateful to those who share my journey.

Peter's got it all figured out. I'm getting there and now I know—someday I'll have it all figured out too.

DO NOT STAND AT MY GRAVE AND WEEP

Do not stand at my grave and weep,
I am not there, I do not sleep.

I am a thousand winds that blow,
I am the softly falling snow,
I am the gently showering rain,
I am the fields of ripening grain.

I am in the morning hush,
I am in the graceful rush
of beautiful birds in circling flight
I am the starshine of the night.

I am in the flowers that bloom
I am in a quiet room,
I am in the birds that sing,
I am in each lovely thing.

Do not stand at my grave and cry,
I am not there—

I do not die!

Mary E. Frye 1937